OPEN MIND, OPEN HEART

By the same author

Invitation to Love
The Mystery of Christ

OPEN MIND, OPEN HEART

The Contemplative Dimension of the Gospel

THOMAS KEATING

ELEMENT
Shaftesbury, Dorset ● Rockport, Massachusetts
Brisbane, Queensland

© 1986 and 1992 St. Benedict's Monastery

First published in the USA in 1986 by Amity House, Inc.

Published in the U.S.A. in 1991 by Element Inc.
42 Broadway, Rockport, MA 01966

Published in Great Britain in 1992 by Element Books Limited
Longmead, Shaftesbury, Dorset

First Element printing April 1991, Reprinted July 1991
New edition January 1992, Reprinted April 1992 and August 1992
Reprinted April and October 1993

Published in Australia by Element Books Limited for
Jacaranda Wiley Limited, 33 Park Road, Milton, Brisbane 4064

Cover illustration 'The Gisela Cross' courtesy of The Ancient Art and
Architecture Collection

Printed in the United States of America

"Dimensions of Contemplative Prayer" first appeared as "Prayer in the Spirit" in
Hosanna, Vol. 1, No. 2 (1983). Used by permission. "An Overview of the History
of Contemplative Prayer in the Christian Tradition" first appeared as
"Contemplative Prayer in the Christian Tradition" in America. Copyright 1978 by
America Press, Inc., 106 West 56th Street, New York, New York 10019. Reprinted
with permission.

For information regarding written or taped materials on centering prayer,
introductory workshops and retreats, please write to Contemplative Outreach Ltd.,
National Office, P.O. Box 737, Butler, N.J. 07405

Library of Congress Cataloging-in-Publication Data
Keating, Thomas
    Open mind, open heart: the contemplative dimension of the Gospel
    Thomas Keating
    Originally published: Warwick, N.Y.: Amity House, 1986.
    1. Contemplation.   2. Prayer.   I. Title.
BV5091.C7K42 1991
248.3'4–dc20 90–86261
86261

British Library Cataloguing in publication data available

ISBN: 1–85230–221–6

Contents

Paraphrase of the Hymn *Veni Sancti Spiritus* *1*

Introduction *3*

1. What Contemplation Is Not *5*

2. Dimensions of Contemplative Prayer *13*

3. The History of Contemplative Prayer
   in the Christian Tradition *19*

4. First steps in Centering Prayer *33*

5. The Sacred Word as Symbol *43*

6. The Ordinary Kinds of Thoughts *53*

7. The Birth of Spiritual Attentiveness *71*

8. The More Subtle Kinds of Thoughts *81*

9. The Unloading of the Unconscious *93*

10. Summary of the Centering Prayer Method *109*

11. The Intensive Centering Prayer Experience *117*

12. Methods of Extending the Effects
    of Contemplative Prayer into Daily Life *123*

13. Guidelines for Christian Life,
Growth and Transformation *127*

Appendices

The Active Prayer   *133*

The Weekly Support Group   *135*

A Meditation   *136*

The Essentials   *138*

A Brief History   *143*

Glossary   *145*

PRAYER TO THE HOLY SPIRIT

Inspired by the Latin hymn *Veni Sancti Spiritus*

Come, Holy Spirit, pour out of the depths of the Trinity a ray of Your Light—that Light which enlightens our minds and, at the same time, strengthens our wills to pursue the Light.

Come, Father of the poor, the poor in spirit, whom You love to fill with the fullness of God.

You are not only Giver of gifts, but Giver of Yourself, the supreme Gift—*the* Gift of the Father and the Son.

You are the best consoler! What a charming Guest You make! Your conversation, though all in silence, is sweetness itself. How refreshing Your consolation! Soothing like a caress. In an instant You dissipate all doubt and sadness.

In the labor of fighting temptation, you are there promising victory. Your presence *is* our victory. You gently coax our timid hearts to trust in You.

In the greatest of labors, the struggle of self-surrender, You are our repose—our peace in the depth of our souls.

In the heat of battle, Your breath is cooling, calming our rebellious passions, quieting our fears when it looks like defeat. You dry our tears when we fall. It is You who give the grace of compunction and the sure hope of pardon.

1

Oh deliriously happy Light! Fill to the uttermost recesses the hearts of Your faithful children!

Without You, there is no divine life in us, no virtue at all. If Your breath is cut off, our spirit perishes; nor can it live again until You press Your lips to our mouths and breathe into them the breath of life.

Your touch is as dew, but You act with a strong hand. Gentle as the softest breeze, You are also in the whirlwind.

Like a giant furnace blast, You dry up all our faculties—but only to melt the hardness of our hearts.

You cast us before You like dead leaves in the winter's gale—but only to set our feet upon the narrow way.

Now, as a mighty Wind coming, pour down torrents to wash away our sins. Drench with grace our dried out hearts. Soothe the wounds You have cauterized.

Give to all who trust in You—with that true trust which only You can give—Your seven sacred Gifts.

Grant the reward of virtue; that is, Your very Self! Grant perseverance to the end! And then, everlasting joy!

Amen

Introduction

Today the Christian churches find themselves with a marvelous opportunity. Many sincere believers are eager to experience contemplative prayer. Along with this aspiration, there is a growing expectation that the leaders of local communities be able to teach the Gospel out of personal experience of contemplative prayer. This could happen if the training of future priests and ministers places formation in prayer and spirituality on an equal footing with academic training. It could also happen if spiritual teaching becomes a regular part of the lay ministry. In any case, until spiritual leadership becomes a reality in Christian circles, many will continue to look to other religious traditions for the spiritual experience they are not finding in their own churches. If there were a widespread renewal of the preaching and practice of the contemplative dimension of the Gospel, the reunion of the Christian churches would become a real possibility, dialogue with the other world religions would have a firm basis in spiritual experience, and the religions of the world would bear a clearer witness to the human values they hold in common.

Centering prayer is an effort to renew the teaching of the Christian tradition on contemplative prayer. It is an attempt to present that tradition in an up-to-date form and to put a certain order and method into it. Like the word *contemplation*, the term *centering prayer* has come to have a variety of meanings. For the sake of clarity it seems best to reserve the

3

term *centering prayer* for the specific method of preparing for the gift of contemplation (described in Chapter Three) and to return to the traditional term *contemplative prayer* when describing its development under the more direct inspiration of the Spirit.

This book has grown out of a number of seminars on the practice of centering prayer and incorporates the specific questions of participants coming from different levels of experience. The concerns expressed by the participants spring from the developing practice of centering prayer. Thus the questions that arise after some months of daily practice are different from those that arise in the first few weeks. The questioner is often asking more than the actual question contains. The responses are aimed at facilitating the listening process initiated by the method of centering prayer. Together with the presentations, they gradually weave a conceptual background for contemplative practice.

Contemplative prayer is a process of interior transformation, a conversation initiated by God and leading, if we consent, to divine union. One's way of seeing reality changes in this process. A restructuring of consciousness takes place which empowers one to perceive, relate and respond with increasing sensitivity to the divine presence in, through, and beyond everything that exists.

CHAPTER ONE

What Contemplation Is Not

There is much popular misinformation in people's minds about what contemplation is. Saying what it is not may help to put a perspective on what it is.

The first thing contemplation is not is a relaxation exercise. It may bring relaxation, but that is strictly a side effect. It is primarily relationship, hence, intentionality. It is not a technique, it is prayer. When we say, "Let us pray", we mean, "Let us enter into a relationship with God", or, "Let us deepen the relationship we have", or, "Let us exercise our relationship with God". Centering prayer is a method of moving our developing relationship with God to the level of pure faith. Pure faith is faith that is moving beyond the mental egoic level of discursive meditation and particular acts to the intuitive level of contemplation. Centering prayer is not designed to bring you to a "high" such as you might obtain by ingesting Peyote or LSD. It is not a form of self-hypnosis. It is simply a method leading to contemplative prayer. In this perspective, it is the first rung on the ladder of contemplative prayer.

The second thing that contemplative prayer is not is a charismatic gift. The charisms enumerated by Paul have been renewed in our time. These gifts are designed for the building up of the community. One may be a contemplative and a charismatic at the same time. And one may not be a contemplative and still have one or more of the charismatic gifts. In other words, there is not necessarily a connection between the two. Contemplative prayer depends on the growth of faith, hope, and divine love, and deals with the purification, healing, and sanctification of the substance of the soul and its faculties. The charismatic gifts are given for the building up of the local community and may be given to people who are not necessarily advanced in the spiritual journey. The gift of tongues is the one gift that may be given primarily for one's personal sanctification. It is a kind of introduction to contemplative prayer because, when praying in tongues, one doesn't know what one is saying.

Another gift is the ability to communicate the experience of *resting in the Spirit*. If you have already had some experience of contemplation, you would recognize it as the gift of infused recollection or perhaps even the prayer of quiet. You can resist it if you want to. If you accept it, you feel a mild suspension of your ordinary sense faculties and you slip to the floor. If people have never experienced this kind of prayer before, they go down with great delight and stay down as long as they can. I once saw a young man fall backwards horizontally as if he were doing a back dive into a swimming pool. He bounced off a little bench, landed on the floor with a terrific crash, and jumped up, completely unhurt.

Apart from the gift of tongues, the charismatic gifts are clearly given for the good of others. They include the interpretation of tongues, prophecy, healing, administration, the word of wisdom, and inspired teaching. Prophecy can exist in people who are not holy at all. A classical example is the prophet Balaam, who prophesied what the King wanted to hear rather than what God had commanded him to say. There were many false prophets in Old Testament times. Since charismatic gifts are frequent in our time and people tend to get excited about them, it is important to realize that they are not an indication either of holiness or of an advanced stage of prayer. They are not the same as contemplative prayer and do not automatically sanctify the people who have them. On the contrary, if one is attached to them, they are a hindrance to one's spiritual development. Even in the exercise of charismatic gifts, emotional programming is at work. According to Catholic tradition, the straight and narrow path of contemplative prayer is the surest and safest path to holiness. The charismatic gifts are accidental or secondary to that path. Obviously, if one has such gifts, one has to integrate them into one's spiritual journey. But if one doesn't have them, there is no reason to think that one is not progressing. The process of transformation depends on the growth of faith, hope, and divine love.

Contemplative prayer is the fruit of that growth and furthers it. Right now the charismatic renewal is in great need of the traditional teaching of the Church on contemplative prayer so that charismatic prayer groups may move on to a new dimension in their relationship with the Holy Spirit. They should introduce periods of silence into the prayer meetings so that shared prayer becomes grounded in the practice of interior silence and contemplation. There is a movement to do precisely that in many prayer groups. If this development fails to take place, the groups risk stagnation. Nothing can stand still on the spiritual journey. These groups need the further growth that the practice of contemplative prayer is meant to provide.

The third thing that contemplative prayer is not is parapsychological phenomena such as precognition, knowledge of events at a distance, control over bodily processes such as heartbeat and breathing, out-of-body experiences, levitation, and other extraordinary sensory or psychic phenomena. The psychic level of consciousness is one level above the mental egoic stage, which is the general level of present human development.

In any case, psychic phenomena are like the frosting on a cake and we cannot survive on frosting alone. We should not overestimate psychic gifts, therefore, or think that holiness manifests itself in extraordinary psychic phenomena. Such manifestations, including levitation, locutions, and visions of various kinds, have been sensational in the lives of some of the saints. Teresa of Avila and John of the Cross, for example, had these experiences. The Christian tradition has consistently counseled avoiding extraordinary gifts whenever possible because it is difficult to remain humble when you have them. Experience teaches that the more extraordinary the gifts, the harder it is to be detached from them. It is easy to take secret satisfaction in the fact that God is giving you special gifts, especially when they are obvious to others.

I have noticed a significant increase in the number of persons experiencing psychic gifts in recent years. In one year alone, I met six people with out-of-body experiences. While asleep or praying, they experienced leaving their body and moving around the house. One man living in Colorado unwittingly found himself in his old home in Massachusetts. No matter how powerful these parapsychological phenomena may be, we should not allow ourselves to be pulled off center by them or to be distracted from our time of prayer. If we wait patiently the phenomenon will pass. If we are doing centering prayer, we should return to the sacred word.

There are actually methods to develop direct control over physiological functions like our breath, heartbeat, and body temperature. I once heard about a young man who had been reading about controlled breathing. Although he knew how to stop breathing, unfortunately he had neglected to read the chapter on how to start breathing again. He never woke up. If you are interested in psychic phenomena, be sure to practice them under an approved master.

Unusual physiological or psychic powers appear to be innate human capacities that can be developed by practicing certain disciplines. But they have nothing to do with holiness or the growth of our relationship to God. To regard them as a sign of great spiritual development is a mistake.

Joseph of Cupertino, a Franciscan friar, was one of the most sensational levitators of all time. He was so much in love with God that at one period in his life whenever he heard the word *God* he would start rising. When he was in church, he would go right up to the ceiling. This was a little distracting for the other brothers in the community and for those who came to worship. One incident that is well authenticated is worth mentioning. The friars were trying to place a huge cross atop a 100-foot steeple on the church. As often happens with levitators, Joseph uttered a loud cry of delight while taking off. He grabbed the cross, which weighed half a ton, flew to the top of the steeple, put it in place and then returned to earth. His superiors took a dim view of his extraordinary behavior and ordered him to desist. There is a certain amount of self in the exercise of any kind of sensational gift, including the most spiritual. When Joseph was ordered to stop levitating, he went into a deep depression. In his case this was clearly the night of the spirit. And that is what made him a saint, not his flying. Airplanes and birds can do that.

In ways often undiscernible to human beings, God allows parapsychological phenomena to operate, or not to operate, as he sees fit.

In the fourteenth century Vincent Ferrer, one of the great wonder workers of his time, was preaching that the end of the world was at hand. On one occasion a man who was being taken for burial was brought to him. Vincent had been preaching his usual doomsday message, so he took this occasion to warn his listeners that the world was coming to an end soon, and to say that as proof of his warning, he would raise this man from the dead. The dead man stood up. But the world did not come to an end. All prophecy is conditional. God does not commit himself to follow through on His threats. He reserves the right to change His mind if people respond by amending their lives. The prophet often gets left holding the bag; it's one of his occupational hazards.

The fourth thing contemplation is not is mystical phenomena. By mystical phenomena, I mean bodily ecstasy, external and internal visions, external words, words spoken in the imagination and words impressed upon one's spirit when any of these are the work of God's special grace in the soul. John of the Cross in *The Ascent to Mt. Carmel* considers every conceivable spiritual phenomenon from the most exterior to the most interior and commands his disciples to reject them all. Pure faith, according to him, is the proximate means of union with God.

External visions and voices can be misunderstood. Even saints have misunderstood what God has said to them. Divine communications of an intelligible kind have to be filtered through the human psyche and one's cultural conditioning. In those who are led by this path, such communications are probably authentic eighty per cent of the time but inauthentic the other twenty per cent. Since one can never tell which percentage group a particular communication belongs to, if one follows these communications without discretion, one can get into all kinds of trouble. There is no guarantee that any particular communication to an individual is actually coming from God. Even if it is, it is almost certain to be distorted by one's imagination, preconceived ideas or emotional programming, any one of which can modify or subtly change the communication. The story of a saint who was promised by God that she would die a martyr's death is a classical example. She did indeed die a holy death, but in bed. As she lay dying, she was tempted to think, "Is God faithful to his promise?" Of course He is faithful to His promise. But he doesn't guarantee that we understand Him correctly when He communicates on the level of the imagination or the reason. God meant that she would die with the same degree of love as a martyr of blood. Her martyrdom of conscience was the equivalent in His eyes to the martyrdom of blood. God does not bind Himself to the literal interpretation of His messages. If we take literally what is said, even when what we understand to be a voice from Heaven orders us to do so, we stand a good chance of deceiving ourselves. If we could just return to the sacred word, we would save ourselves so much trouble.

All the sacraments are greater than any vision. This is not to say that visions may not have a purpose in our lives, but as John of the Cross teaches, a genuine communication from God accomplishes its purpose instantly. Reflecting on it does not make it any better—but often distorts it—by losing its original clarity. This does not prevent one from mentioning it to a prudent spiritual director to make sure one does not take it too seriously or too lightly. If one is told by God to do something, it is especially important not to do anything without first discerning the matter carefully with an experienced spiritual director.

Much more reliable than visions, locutions, or the process of reasoning are the inner impressions that the Spirit suggests in prayer and to which we feel gently but consistently inclined. The more important the event, the more we have to listen to sound reason and consult a spiritual director. God's will is not always easy to discern; we have to observe all the indications of it and then decide. In the struggle for certitude however, we perceive more clearly what the obstacles are in ourselves to recognizing His will.

We come now to the question of mystical graces. They are the hardest to distinguish because they are so intertwined with our psyche. By mystical graces I mean the inflowing of God's presence into our faculties or the radiance of His presence when it spontaneously overtakes us. The levels of mystical prayer have been well described by Teresa of Avila and John of the Cross. They include infused recollection, the prayer of quiet, the prayer of union, the prayer of full union, and finally, the transforming union. I prefer to use the terms *contemplation* and *mysticism* to mean the same thing and to distinguish mystical graces from the essence of mystical prayer. Is it possible to be a contemplative and attain the transforming union without going through the experience of the mystical graces just described?

This is a question that has puzzled me over the years because contemplation as the experience of the inflow of God's grace has generally been considered a necessary sign of the gift of contemplative prayer. However, I continue to meet people who are very advanced in the spiritual journey who insist that they have never had the grace of contemplative prayer as a felt experience of God. Having spent thirty or forty years in a monastery or convent in order to become contemplatives, some of these people are tempted at times to feel that their lives have been a gigantic failure. They wind up in their sixties or seventies believing that since they never had such an experience, they must have done something wrong. Here are people who have given their whole lives to the service of Christ and yet have no internal assurance of having had even the least mystical grace.

The first few times I listened to these people's experiences, I thought perhaps they had never been properly instructed in contemplative prayer, or maybe they had received touches of it in their early religious life and either forgot about it or got used to it. But I have since changed my mind. I am convinced that it is a mistake to identify the *experience* of contemplative prayer with contemplative prayer itself, which transcends any impression of God's radiating or inflowing presence. I was pleased to see my experience articulated by Ruth Burroughs, a Carmelite nun who has lived her religious life without any experiential awareness of the radiance of God's presence. In *Guidelines to Mystical Prayer*, she proposes the distinction of *lights on* mysticism and *lights off* mysticism. This would explain how, for many persons, their whole contemplative journey is completely hidden from them until their final transformation. This Carmelite nun had two friends, one with a very exuberant mystical life, in an active order and the other a nun in her own cloistered convent who had never enjoyed any conscious experience of contemplative prayer although she had faithfully practiced the discipline of contemplative prayer for forty years. Both wound up in transforming union. Ruth Burroughs extrapolates that mystical grace may be a charism that certain mystics are given in order to explain the spiritual path to others. In any case, her hypothesis rests on the assumption that the essence of mysticism is the path of pure faith. Pure faith, according to John of the Cross, is a ray of darkness to the soul. There is no faculty that can perceive it. One can be having this "experience" on the deepest level beyond the power of any faculty to perceive it. One can only remark its presence by its fruits in one's life. God can be beaming that ray of darkness into someone who is faithful to prayer without his or her being conscious of it at all. In any case, the people in my experience who have the most exuberant mystical lives are married or in the active ministry. Less than five per cent of cloistered contemplatives that I know have the mystical experiences that Teresa or John of the Cross describe. They generally experience the night of sense, and a few experience the night of spirit. Their consolations are few and far between. Those who are in the world doubtless need more help in order to survive. Perhaps God does not help cloistered folks in the same way because He has decided that they have enough support from the structures of their enclosed lifestyle.

What is the essence of contemplative prayer? The way of pure faith. Nothing else. You do not have to feel it, but you have to practice it.

CHAPTER TWO

Dimensions of Contemplative Prayer

Contemplative prayer is the world in which God can do anything. To move into that realm is the greatest adventure. It is to be open to the Infinite and hence to infinite possibilities. Our private, self-made worlds come to an end; a new world appears within and around us and the impossible becomes an everyday experience. Yet the world that prayer reveals is barely noticeable in the ordinary course of events.

Christian life and growth are founded on faith in our own basic goodness, in the being that God has given us with its transcendent potential. This gift of being is our true Self. Through our consent by faith, Christ is born in us and He and our true Self become one. Our awakening to the presence and action of the Spirit is the unfolding of Christ's resurrection in us.

All true prayer is based on the conviction of the presence of the Spirit in us and of his unfailing and continual inspiration. Every prayer in this sense is prayer in the Spirit. Still, it seems more accurate to reserve the term *prayer in the Spirit*, for that prayer in which the inspiration of the Spirit is given directly to our spirit without the intermediary of our own reflections or acts of will. In other words, the Spirit prays in us and we consent. The traditional term for this kind of prayer is *contemplation*.

We should distinguish *contemplative prayer* from *contemplative life*. The former is an experience or series of experiences leading to the abiding state of union with God. The term *contemplative life* should be reserved for the abiding state of divine union itself, in which one is moved both in prayer and in action by the Spirit.

The root of prayer is interior silence. We may think of prayer as thoughts or feelings expressed in words, but this is only one of its forms. "Prayer," according to Evagrius, "is the laying aside of thoughts".[1] This definition presupposes that there *are* thoughts. Contemplative prayer is not so much the absence of thoughts as detachment from them. It is the opening of mind and heart, body and emotions—our whole being—to God, the Ultimate Mystery, beyond words, thoughts and emotions— beyond, in other words, the psychological content of the present moment. We do not deny or repress what is in our consciousness. We simply accept the fact of whatever is there and go beyond it, not by effort, but by letting go of whatever is there.

According to the Baltimore catechism, "Prayer is the raising of the mind and heart to God." In using this ancient formula it is important to keep in mind that it is not *we* who do the lifting. In every kind of prayer the raising of the mind and heart to God can be the work only of the Spirit. In prayer inspired by the Spirit we let ourselves flow with the lifting movement and drop all reflection. Reflection is an important preliminary to prayer, but it is not prayer. Prayer is not only the offering of interior acts to God: it is the offering of ourselves, of who and what we are.

The action of the Spirit might be compared to a skillful nurse teaching the adopted children of a wealthy household how to behave in their new home. Like waifs pulled in off the street and seated at the banquet table in the elegant dining hall, we require a lot of time to learn and practice the proper table manners. Because of our earthy background, we tend to put our muddy feet on the table, break the chinaware and spill the soup in our laps. To assimilate the values of our new home, profound changes in our attitudes and behavioral patterns are required. For this reason we may experience our nurse as constraining in the beginning and heavy on the "don'ts". And yet she always seems to be encouraging in the midst of correction; never condemnatory, never judgmental, always inviting us to amendment of life. The practice of contemplative prayer is an education imparted by the Spirit.

Our participation in this educational process is what Christian tradi-

1. Evagrius, *De Oratione* 70 (PG 79, 1181C).

tion calls self-denial. Jesus said, "Unless you deny your inmost self and take up the cross, you cannot be my disciple." (Mark 8:34) Denial of our *inmost self* includes detachment from the habitual functioning of our intellect and will, which are our inmost faculties. This may require letting go not only of ordinary thoughts during prayer, but also of our most devout reflections and aspirations insofar as we treat them as indispensable means of going to God.

The nature of the human mind is to simplify what it thinks about. Thus a single thought can sum up an immense wealth of reflection. The thought itself becomes a *presence*, an act of attention rather than of understanding. If we apply this principle to the person of Jesus, we can see that this kind of attention does not in any way exclude his humanity. Our attention is simply given to the *presence* of Jesus, the divine-human being, without adverting to any particular detail of his person.

Contemplative prayer is part of a dynamic process that evolves through personal relationship rather than by strategy. At the same time a reasonable amount of organization in one's prayer and lifestyle advances the process, just as wholesome food and exercise help youngsters grow to physical maturity.

One of the first effects of contemplative prayer is the release of the energies of the unconscious. This process gives rise to two different psychological states: the experience of personal development in the form of spiritual consolation, charismatic gifts or psychic powers; and the experience of human weakness through humiliating self-knowledge. Self-knowledge is the traditional term for the coming to consciousness of the dark side of one's personality. The release of these two kinds of unconscious energies needs to be safeguarded by well-established habits of dedication to God and concern for others. Otherwise, if one enjoys some form of spiritual consolation or development one may inflate with pride; or if one feels crushed by the realization of one's spiritual impoverishment, one may collapse into discouragement or even despair. The cultivation of habits of dedication to God and of service to others is the indispensable means of stabilizing the mind in the face of emotionally charged thoughts, whether of self-exaltation or of self-depreciation.

Dedication to God is developed by commitment to one's spiritual practices for God's sake. Service to others is the outgoing movement of the heart prompted by compassion. It neutralizes the deep-rooted tendency to become preoccupied with our own spiritual journey and how we are doing. The habit of service to others is developed by trying to please God in what we do and by exercising compassion for others, beginning with those with whom we live. To accept everyone unconditionally is to fulfill the commandment to "love your neighbor as yourself". (Mark 12:31) It is a practical way of bearing one another's burdens. (Galatians 6:2) Refusing to judge even in the face of persecution is to fulfill the commandment to love one another "as I have loved you" (John 13:34) and to lay down one's life for one's friends. (John 15:13)

Habits of dedication to God and service to others form the two sides of a channel through which the energies of the unconscious can be released without submerging the psyche in the floodwaters of chaotic emotions. On the contrary, when these energies flow in orderly fashion between the banks of dedication and service, they will raise us to higher levels of spiritual perception, understanding, and selfless love.

These two stabilizing dispositions prepare the nervous system and body to receive the purifying and sanctifying light of the Spirit. They enable us to discern thoughts and emotions as they arise before they reach the stage of attachment or quasi-compulsion. As independence from the thralldom of habitual thoughts and desires grows, we are able to enter into contemplative prayer with a quiet mind.

Detachment is the goal of self-denial. It is the nonpossessive attitude toward all of reality, the disposition that strikes at the root of the false self system. The false self is a monumental illusion, a load of habitual thinking patterns and emotional routines that are stored in the brain and nervous system. Like programs in a computer, they tend to reactivate every time a particular life situation pushes the appropriate button. The false self even insinuates that its subtle purposes are religiously motivated. Genuine religious attitudes come from God, not from the false self. By means of contemplative prayer the Spirit heals the roots of self-centeredness and becomes the source of our conscious activity. To act spontaneously under the Spirit's influence rather than under the influence of the false self, the emotional programming of the past has to be erased and replaced. *The practice of virtue* is the traditional term for erasing the old programs and writing new programs based on the values of the Gospel.

Jesus in His divinity is the source of contemplation. When the presence of the Divine is experienced as overwhelming, we are inwardly compelled to contemplate. Such was the situation of the apostles on Mount Tabor when they witnessed the glory of God shining through the humanity of Jesus. They fell on their faces. Our experiences of God, however, are not God as He is in Himself. God as He is in Himself cannot be experienced empirically, conceptually or spiritually. He is beyond experiences of any kind. This does not mean that He is not *in* sacred experiences, but that He *transcends* them. To put this insight in another way, He leads us by means of sacred experiences to the experience of emptiness. Anything that we perceive of God can only be a radiance of His presence and not God as He is Himself. When the divine light strikes the human mind, it breaks down into many aspects just as a ray of ordinary light, when it strikes a prism, breaks down into the varied colors of the spectrum. There is nothing wrong with distinguishing different aspects of the Ultimate Mystery, but it would be a mistake to identify them with the inaccessible Light. The attraction to let go of spiritual consolation in order to let God act with complete freedom is the persistent attraction of the Spirit. The more one lets go, the stronger the presence of the Spirit becomes. The Ultimate Mystery becomes the Ultimate Presence.

The Spirit speaks to our conscience through scripture and through the events of daily life. Reflection on these two sources of personal encounter and the dismantling of the emotional programming of the past prepare the psyche to listen at more refined levels of attention. The Spirit then begins to address our conscience from that deep source within us which is our true Self. This is contemplation properly so-called.

This pattern is exemplified in the Transfiguration. Jesus took with him the three disciples who were best prepared to receive the grace of contemplation; that is, the ones who had made the most headway in changing their hearts. God approached them through their senses by means of the vision on the mountain. At first they were overawed and delighted. Peter wanted to remain there forever. Suddenly a cloud covered them, hiding the vision and leaving their senses empty and quiet, yet attentive and alert. The gesture of falling on their faces accurately expressed their state of mind. It was a posture of adoration, gratitude, and love all rolled into one. The voice from heaven awakened their consciousness to the presence of the Spirit, who had always been speaking within them, but whom until then they had never been able to hear. Their interior emptiness was filled with the luminous presence of the divine. At Jesus' touch they returned to their ordinary perceptions and saw him as he was before but with the transformed consciousness of faith. They no longer saw him as a mere human being. Their receptive and active faculties had been unified by the Spirit; the interior and exterior word of God had become one. For those who have attained this consciousness, daily life is a continual and increasing revelation of God. The words they hear in scripture and in the liturgy confirm what they have learned through the prayer that is contemplation.

CHAPTER THREE

The History of Contemplative Prayer in the Christian Tradition

A positive attitude toward contemplation characterized the first fifteen centuries of the Christian era. Unfortunately, a negative attitude has prevailed from the sixteenth century onward. To understand the situation in which we find our churches today in regard to religious experience, an overview of the history of contemplative prayer may prove helpful.

The word *contemplation* is an ambiguous term because over the centuries it has acquired several different meanings. To emphasize the experiential knowledge of God, the Greek Bible used the word *gnosis* to translate the Hebrew *da'ath*, a much stronger term that implies an intimate kind of knowledge involving the whole person, not just the mind.

St. Paul used the word *gnosis* in his Epistles to refer to the knowledge of God proper to those who love Him. He constantly asked for this intimate knowledge for his disciples and prayed for it as if it were an indispensable element for the full development of Christian life.

The Greek Fathers, especially Clement of Alexandria, Origen and Gregory of Nyssa, borrowed from the Neoplatonists the term *theoria*. This originally meant the intellectual vision of truth, which the Greek philosophers regarded as the supreme activity of the person of wisdom. To this technical term the Fathers added the meaning of the Hebrew *da'ath*, that is, the kind of experiential knowledge that comes through love. It was with this expanded understanding of the term that *theoria* was translated into

19

the Latin *contemplatio* and handed down to us in the Christian tradition.

This tradition was summed up by Gregory the Great at the end of the Sixth Century when he described contemplation as the knowledge of God that is impregnated with love. For Gregory, contemplation is the fruit of reflection on the word of God in scripture and at the same time a gift of God. It is a *resting* in God. In this resting or stillness the mind and heart are not actively seeking Him but are beginning to experience, to taste, what they have been seeking. This places them in a state of tranquility and profound interior peace. This state is not the suspension of all action, but the mingling of a few simple acts of will to sustain one's attention to God with the loving experience of God's presence.

This meaning of contemplation as the knowledge of God based on the intimate experience of His presence remained the same until the end of the Middle Ages. Ascetical disciplines were always directed toward contemplation as the proper goal of every spiritual practice.

The method of prayer proposed for lay persons and monastics alike in the first Christian centuries was called *lectio divina*, literally, "divine reading", a practice that involved reading scripture, or more exactly, listening to it. Monastics would repeat the words of the sacred text with their lips so that the body itself entered into the process. They sought to cultivate through *lectio divina* the capacity to listen at ever deeper levels of inward attention. Prayer was their response to the God to whom they were listening in scripture and giving praise in the liturgy.

The reflective part, pondering upon the words of the sacred text, was called *meditatio*, "meditation". The spontaneous movement of the will in response to these reflections was called *oratio*, "affective prayer". As these reflections and acts of will simplified, one moved on to a state of resting in the presence of God, and that is what was meant by *contemplatio*, "contemplation".

These three acts—discursive meditation, affective prayer and contemplation—might all take place during the same period of prayer. They were interwoven one into the other. Like the angels ascending and descending on Jacob's ladder, one's attention was expected to go up and down the ladder of consciousness. Sometimes one would praise the Lord with one's lips, sometimes with one's thoughts, sometimes with acts of will, and sometimes with the rapt attention of contemplation. Contemplation was regarded as the normal development of listening to the word of God. The approach to God was not compartmentalized into discursive meditation, affective

prayer and contemplation. The term *mental prayer*, with its distinct categories, did not exist in Christian tradition prior to the Sixteenth Century.

Around the Twelfth Century a marked development in religious thought
took place. The great schools of theology were founded. It was the birth
of precise analysis in regard to concepts, division into genera and species,
and definitions and classifications. This growing capacity for analysis was
a significant development of the human mind. Unfortunately this passion
for analysis in theology was later to be transferred to the practice of prayer
and bring to an end the simple, spontaneous prayer of the Middle Ages
based on *lectio divina* with its opening to contemplation. Spiritual masters
of the Twelfth Century, like Bernard of Clairvaux, Hugh and Richard of
St. Victor, and William of St. Thierry, were developing a theological understanding of prayer and contemplation. In the Thirteenth Century methods
of meditation based on their teaching were popularized by the Franciscans.

During the Fourteenth and Fifteenth Centuries, the Black Death and
the Hundred Years' War decimated cities, towns and religious communities
while nominalism and the Great Schism brought on a general decadence
in morals and spirituality. A movement of renewal, called Devotio Moderna,
arose in the Low Countries around 1380 and spread to Italy, France and
Spain in response to the widespread need for reform. In an age when institutions and structures of all kinds were crumbling, the movement of
Devotio Moderna sought to utilize the moral power issuing from prayer as
a means of self-discipline. By the end of the Fifteenth Century, methods
of mental prayer, properly so-called, were elaborated, becoming more and
more complicated and systematized as time went on. But even while this
proliferation of systematic methods of prayer was taking place, contemplation was still presented as the ultimate goal of spiritual practice.

As the Sixteenth Century progressed, mental prayer came to be divided
into discursive meditation if thoughts predominated; affective prayer if the
emphasis was on acts of the will; and contemplation if graces infused by
God were predominant. Discursive meditation, affective prayer, and contemplation were no longer different acts found in a single period of prayer,
but distinct forms of prayer, each with its own proper aim, method and
purpose. This division of the development of prayer into compartmentalized
units entirely separate from one another helped to further the incorrect
notion that contemplation was an extraordinary grace reserved to the few.
The possibility of prayer opening out into contemplation tended to be
regarded as very unlikely. The organic development of prayer toward con-

templation did not fit into the approved categories and was therefore discouraged.

At the same time that the living tradition of Christian contemplation was diminishing, the Renaissance brought new challenges for the spiritual life. No longer were the social milieu and religious institutions supportive of the individual. There was the need to reconquer the world for Christ in the face of the pagan elements that were taking over Christendom. It was not surprising that new forms of prayer should appear that were ordered to an apostolic ministry. The new emphasis on apostolic life required a transformation of the forms of spirituality hitherto transmitted by monastics and mendicants. The genius and contemplative experience of Ignatius of Loyola led him to channel the contemplative tradition, which was in danger of being lost, into a form appropriate to the new age.

The *Spiritual Exercises of Saint Ignatius*, composed between 1522 and 1526, is extremely important in order to understand the present state of spirituality in the Roman Catholic Church. Three methods of prayer are proposed in the *Spiritual Exercises*. The discursive meditations prescribed for the first week are made according to the method of the three powers: memory, intellect and will. The memory is to recall the point chosen beforehand as the subject of the discursive meditation. The intellect is to reflect on the lessons one wants to draw from that point. The will is to make resolutions based on that point in order to put the lessons into practice. Thus, one is led to reformation of life.

The word *contemplation*, as it is used in the *Spiritual Exercises*, has a meaning different from the traditional one. It consists of gazing upon a concrete object of the imagination: seeing the persons in the Gospel as if they were present, hearing what they are saying, relating and responding to their words and actions. This method, prescribed for the second week, is aimed at developing affective prayer.

The third method of prayer in the *Spiritual Exercises* is called the application of the five senses. It consists of successively applying in spirit the five senses to the subject of the meditation. This method is designed to dispose beginners to contemplation in the traditional sense of the term and to develop the spiritual senses in those who are already advanced in prayer.

Thus, Ignatius did not propose only one method of prayer. The unfortunate tendency to reduce the *Spiritual Exercises* to a method of discursive meditation seems to stem from the Jesuits themselves. In 1574 Everard Mercurian, the Father General of the Jesuits, in a directive to the Spanish province of the Society, forbade the practice of affective prayer and the application of the five senses. This prohibition was repeated in 1578. The spiritual life of a significant portion of the Society of Jesus was thus limited to a single method of prayer, namely, discursive meditation according to the three powers. The predominantly intellectual character of this meditation continued to grow in importance throughout the Society during the course of the eighteenth and nineteenth centuries. Most manuals of spirituality until well into this century limited instruction to schemas of discursive meditation.

To comprehend the impact of this development on the recent history of Roman Catholic spirituality, we should keep in mind the pervasive influence that the Jesuits exercised as the outstanding representatives of the Counter-Reformation. Many religious congregations founded in the centuries following this period adopted the Constitutions of the Society of Jesus. They received at the same time the spirituality taught and practiced by the Society. Hence they also received the limitations imposed not by Ignatius, but by his less enlightened successors.

Ignatius wished to provide a spiritual formation that was an appropriate antidote to the new secular and individualist spirit of the Renaissance and a form of contemplative prayer adapted to the apostolic needs of his time. The *Spiritual Exercises* were designed to form contemplatives in action. Considering the immense influence of the Society for good, if it's members had been allowed to follow the *Spiritual Exercises* according to Ignatius' original intent, or if they had given more prominence to their own contemplative masters like Fathers Lallemant, Surin, Grou and de Caussade, the present state of spirituality among Roman Catholics might be quite different.

Other events contributed to the hesitation of Roman Catholic authorities to encourage contemplative prayer. One of these was the controversy regarding Quietism, a set of spiritual teachings condemned in 1687 as a species of false mysticism by Innocent XII. The condemned teachings were ingenious. They consisted of making once and for all an act of love for God by which one gave oneself entirely to Him with the intention never to recall this surrender. As long as one never withdrew the intention to belong entirely to God, divine union was assured and no further need for effort either in prayer or outside of it was required. The important distinction between making a one-time intention (however generous) and establishing it as a permanent disposition seems to have passed unnoticed.

A milder form of this doctrine flourished in France in the latter part of the seventeenth century and became known as Semi-Quietism. Bishop Boussuet, chaplain to the court of Louis XIV, was one of the chief enemies of this attenuated form of Quietism and succeeded in having it condemned in France. How much he exaggerated the teaching is difficult to ascertain. In any case, the controversy brought traditional mysticism into disrepute. From then on, reading about mysticism was frowned upon in seminaries and religious communities. According to Henri Bremond in his book *The Literary History of Religious Thought in France*, no mystical writing of any significance occurred during the next several hundred years. The mystical writers of the past were ignored. Even passages from John of the Cross were thought to be suggestive of Quietism, forcing his editors to tone down or expunge certain statements lest they be misunderstood and condemned. The unexpurgated text of his writings appeared only in our own century, four hundred years after its writing.

A further set-back for Christian spirituality was the heresy of Jansenism, which gained momentum during the seventeenth century. Although it, too, was eventually condemned, it left behind a pervasive anti-human attitude that perdured throughout the nineteenth century and into our own time. Jansenism questions the universality of Jesus' saving action as well as the intrinsic goodness of human nature. The pessimistic form of piety which it fostered spread with the emigrés from the French Revolution to English-speaking regions including Ireland and the United States. Since it is largely from French and Irish stock that priests and religious in this country have come, Jansenistic narrowness, together with its distorted asceticism, has deeply affected the psychological climate of our seminaries and religious orders. Priests and religious are still shaking off the last remnants of the negative attitudes that they absorbed in the course of their ascetical formation.

Another unhealthy trend in the modern Church was the excessive emphasis on private devotions, apparitions, and private revelations. This led to the devaluation of the liturgy together with the communitarian values and sense of transcendent mystery which good liturgy engenders. The popular mind continued to regard contemplatives as saints, wonder workers, or at the very least, exceptional people. The true nature of contemplation remained obscure or confused with phenomena such as levitation, locutions, stigmata, and visions, which are strictly accidental to it.

During the nineteenth century there were many saints, but few spoke or wrote about contemplative prayer. There was a renewal of spirituality in Eastern Orthodoxy, but the mainstream of Roman Catholic development was legalistic in character, with a kind of nostalgia for the Middle Ages and for the political influence that the Church exercised at that time.

Abbot Cuthbert Butler sums up the generally accepted ascetical teaching during the eighteenth and nineteenth centuries in his book *Western Mysticism*.

> Except for very unusual vocations, the normal prayer for everyone including contemplative monks and nuns, bishops, priests and laypersons was systematic meditation following a fixed method, which could be one of four: the meditation according to the three powers as laid down in the *Spiritual Exercises of Saint Ignatius*, the method of St. Alphonsus (which was a slight reworking of the *Spiritual Exercises*), the method described by St. Francis de Sales in *An Introduction to the Devout Life*, or the method of St. Sulpice.

These are all methods of discursive meditation. Contemplation was identified with extraordinary phenomena, and was regarded as both miraculous and dangerous, to be admired from a safe distance by the average layperson, priest or religious.

The final nail hammered into the coffin of the traditional teaching was that it would be arrogant to aspire to contemplative prayer. Novices and seminarians were thus presented with a highly truncated view of the spiritual life, one that did not accord with scripture, tradition and the normal experience of growth in prayer. If one attempts to persevere in discursive meditation after the Holy Spirit has called one beyond it, as the Spirit ordinarily does, one is bound to wind up in a state of utter frustration. It is normal for the mind to move through many reflections on the same theme to a single comprehensive view of the whole, then to rest with a simple gaze upon the truth. As devout people moved spontaneously into this development in their prayer, they were up against this negative attitude toward contemplation. They hesitated to go beyond discursive meditation or affective prayer because of the warnings they had been given about the dangers of contemplation. In the end they either gave up mental prayer altogether as something for which they were evidently unsuited, or, through the mercy of God, found some way of persevering in spite of what seemed like insurmountable obstacles.

In any case, the post-Reformation teaching opposed to contemplation was the direct opposite of the earlier tradition. That tradition, taught uninterruptedly for the first fifteen centuries, held that contemplation is the normal evolution of a genuine spiritual life and hence is open to all Christians. These historical factors may help to explain how the traditional spirituality of the West came to be lost in recent centuries and why Vatican II had to address itself to the acute problem of spiritual renewal.

There are two reasons that contemplative prayer is receiving renewed attention in our time. One is that historical and theological studies have rediscovered the integral teaching of John of the Cross and other masters of the spiritual life. The other is the post-World War II challenge from the East. Methods of meditation similar to contemplative prayer in the Christian tradition have proliferated, produced good results, and received much publicity. It is important, according to the *Declaration on the Relationship of the Church to Non-Christian Religions* (Vatican II), to appreciate the values that are present in the teachings of the other great religions of the world. The spiritual disciplines of the East possess a highly developed psychological wisdom. Christian leaders and teachers need to know something about them in order to meet people where they are today. Many serious seekers of truth study the Eastern religions, take courses in them in college or graduate school, and practice forms of meditation inspired and taught by Eastern masters.

The revival of mystical theology in the Roman Catholic Church began with the publication of *The Degrees of the Spiritual Life* by Abbe Saudreau in 1896. He based his research on the teaching of John of the Cross. Subsequent studies have confirmed the wisdom of his choice. John of the Cross teaches that contemplation begins with what he calls the night of sense. This is a no-man's land between one's own activity and the direct inspiration of the Holy Spirit in which it becomes almost impossible to think thoughts that stir up sensible devotion. This is a common experience among those who have practiced discursive meditation over an extended period of time. One reaches the point where there is nothing new to be thought, said, or felt. If one has no subsequent direction in the life of prayer, one will not know what to do except perhaps to get up and walk out. The night of sense is a spiritual growing-up process similar to the transition from childhood to adolescence in chronological life. The emotionalism and sentimentality of childhood are beginning to be laid aside in favor of a more mature relationship with God. In the meantime, because God no longer gives help to the senses or to the reason, these faculties seem to be useless. One is more and more convinced that one can no longer pray at all.

John of the Cross says that all one has to do in this state is to remain at peace, not try to think, and to abide before God with faith in His presence, continually turning to Him as if opening one's eyes to look upon a loved one.

In a remarkable passage in *The Living Flame of Love*[1] in which John of the Cross describes in detail the transition from sensible devotion to spiritual intimacy with God, he says that when one cannot reason discursively or make acts of the will with any satisfaction during prayer, one should give the situation a quiet welcome. One will then begin to feel peace, tranquillity, and strength because God is now feeding the soul directly, giving His grace to the will alone and attracting it mysteriously to Himself. People in this state have great anxiety about whether they are going backward. They think that all the good things they experienced in the first years of their conversion are coming to an end, and if they are asked how their prayer life is, they will throw up their hands in despair. Actually, if questioned further, they reveal that they have a great desire to find some way to pray and they like to be alone with God even though they can't enjoy Him. Thus, it is evident that there is a secret attraction present at a deep level of their psyche. This is the infused element of contemplative prayer. Divine love is the infused element. If it is given a quiet rest, it will grow from a spark into a living flame of love.

John of the Cross says that those who give themselves to God enter very quickly into the night of sense. This interior desert is the beginning of contemplative prayer even though they are not aware of it. The relationship between one's own activity and the infusion of grace is so delicate that one does not usually perceive it right away. Since the night of sense occurs frequently, it is important that spiritual directors be available to help Christians to appreciate and welcome this development and to recognize it by the signs suggested by John of the Cross. If one gets through this transition, one is on the way to becoming a very dedicated and effective Christian, one who is wholly under the guidance of the gifts of the Spirit.

How quickly is "very quickly" in the teaching of John of the Cross? Is it a few years, a few months, a few weeks? He doesn't say. But the idea that one has to undergo years of superhuman trials, be walled up behind

---

1. Stanza III, 26-59.

convent walls or kill oneself with various ascetical practices before one can aspire to contemplation is a Jansenistic attitude or, at the very least, an inadequate presentation of the Christian tradition. On the contrary, the sooner contemplative prayer can be experienced, the sooner one will perceive the direction toward which the spiritual journey is tending. From that intuition will come the motivation to make all the sacrifices required to persevere in the journey.

As the introduction to this book indicates, the questions of participants in seminars on the practice of centering prayer are included in the text where appropriate. The following paragraph forms the first such question. Others appear throughout the text wherever they are thought to be helpful to the reader.

> *The Cloud of Unknowing* has a lot to say about being ready for this movement into contemplative prayer. It presupposes that not everyone is called to this. It gives signs for telling whether you are called or not. Yet today it seems to be offered to everyone, not only by teachers of centering prayer, but also by teachers of Eastern meditation. It is as if it is open to all.

The idea of laypeople pursuing the spiritual path is not something new. It just hasn't been popular in the past thousand years. In the spiritual traditions of the world religions, both East and West, there has been a tendency to isolate seekers, put them in special places, and juxtapose them with people leading family, professional, or business lives in the world. But this distinction is beginning to change. The sages of India, for example, have begun to share their secrets with ordinary folks. In times past one normally had to go into the forest to find a teacher. In the United States and Western Europe, we can now find outstanding teachers of different Eastern spiritual traditions offering advanced teachings to almost anyone who comes along. Lesser expressions of these traditions, unfortunately, are also available. In any case, a movement in the Eastern religions to make esoteric disciplines more available to persons living ordinary lives in the world is occurring.

With regards to the Christian tradition, Origen, a fourth-century exponent of the theological school of Alexandria, considered the Christian community in the world to be the proper place of ascesis. It was only through Anthony's example and Athanasius's report of it that the practice of leaving the world became the standard way to pursue the Christian path to divine union. Anthony had no intention of making this the only way to achieve it, but when mass movements occur, popularizations also take place, and these may fossilize or even caricature a movement. A new wave of spiritual renewal has to arise before the necessary distinctions can again be made. This may take a long time when movements have become institutionalized. The essence of monastic life is not its structures but its interior practice, and the heart of interior practice is contemplative prayer.

In *The Epistle of Privy Counseling*, written toward the end of his life, the author of *The Cloud of Unknowing* acknowledges that the call to contemplative prayer is more common than he had originally thought. In practice I think we can teach people to proceed in tandem toward contemplative prayer, that is, to read and reflect on the word of God in scripture, make aspirations inspired by these reflections, and then to rest in the presence of God. This is how *lectio divina* was practiced in the monasteries of the Middle Ages. The method of centering prayer emphasizes the final phase of *lectio* because it is the phase that has been most neglected in recent times.

My conviction is that if people are never exposed to some kind of non-conceptual prayer, it may never develop at all because of the overly intellectual bias of Western culture and the anticontemplative trend of Christian teaching in recent centuries. Moreover, some experiential taste of interior silence is a great help in understanding what contemplative prayer is all about. Recent ascetical teaching has been extremely cautious. There has been a strong tendency to assume that contemplative prayer was reserved for cloistered religious.

Contemplative prayer raises an important question: Is there something that we can do to prepare ourselves for the gift of contemplation instead of waiting for God to do everything? My acquaintance with Eastern methods of meditation has convinced me that there is. There are ways of calming the mind in the spiritual disciplines of both East and West that can help to lay the groundwork for contemplative prayer.

What is the difference between *lectio divina* and centering prayer?

Lectio is a comprehensive method of communing with God which begins with the reading of a scripture passage. Reflection on the text moves easily into spontaneous prayer (talking to God about what you have read), and finally into resting in the presence of God. Centering prayer is a way of moving from the first three phases of *lectio* to the final one of resting in God.

> St. John of the Cross and St. Teresa advised that one should only discontinue discursive meditation when God takes away one's ability to practice it. How does centering prayer fit in with that tradition?

A certain amount of reflection on the truths of faith to develop basic convictions, which is the work of discursive meditation, is a necessary basis for contemplation. To the objection that we might be introducing con-templative prayer too soon, my answer is that our contemporaries in the Western world have a special problem with discursive meditation because of the ingrained inclination to analyze things beyond all measure, a mind-set that has developed out of the Cartesian-Newtonian world view and that has led to the repression of our intuitive faculties. This conceptual hang-up of modern Western society impedes the spontaneous movement from reflection to spontaneous prayer and from spontaneous prayer to interior silence (wonder and admiration). I think you could do all three in tandem and still be in the tradition of *lectio divina*. If you are practicing *lectio divina*, you don't have to follow any particular order or time schedule. You can follow the inspiration of grace and mull over the text, make particular acts of the will, or move into contemplative prayer at any time. Obviously discursive meditation and affective prayer will predominate in the beginning. But this does not exclude moments of interior silence. If people were encouraged to reflect on scripture and be fully present to the words of the sacred text, and then practice a period of centering prayer, they would actually be in the tradition of *lectio*.

> It's much clearer to me now. Centering prayer sort of compensates for the lack of people's ability in our time to go from *lectio* into contemplation.

Exactly. It is an insight into a contemporary problem and an effort to revive the traditional Christian teaching on contemplative prayer. But more than just a theoretical effort to revive it is required. Some means of expos-ing people to the actual experience is essential to get beyond the intellectual bias that exists. Having observed this bias in people who are already into contemplative prayer, I'm convinced that it is much deeper in our culture than we think. The rush to the East is a symptom of what is lacking in the West. There is a deep spiritual hunger that is not being satisfied in the West.

I have also noticed that those who have been on an Eastern journey feel much more comfortable about the Christian religion when they hear that a tradition of contemplative prayer exists. Centering prayer as a preparation for contemplative prayer is not something that someone invented in our day. Rather it is a means of regaining the traditional teaching on contemplative prayer and of making this teaching better known and more available. The only thing that is new is trying to communicate it in a methodical way. One needs help to get into it and follow-up to sustain and grow in it.

One who has already received the grace of contemplative prayer can deepen it by cultivating interior silence in a consistent and orderly fashion. It is with a view to cultivating interior silence that the method of centering prayer is offered.

CHAPTER FOUR

First Steps in Centering Prayer

Since Vatican II the Roman Catholic Church has been encouraging Catholics to live the fullness of the Christian life without expecting priests, religious or anyone else to do it for them. That implies creativity as well as responsibility on the part of lay people to come up with structures that will enable them to live the contemplative dimensions of the Gospel without a cloister. A cloister does not resolve all the problems of life. There are pitfalls and traps for monks and nuns as well as for other people.

The monastic journey is a special kind of life with its own set of difficulties. For one thing, it puts human relationships under a microscope. Although the trials are not as big as those outside the monastery, they may be more humiliating. Monastics get upset by trifles and can't even claim a good reason for feeling that way.

Divine union is the goal for all Christians. We have been baptised; we receive the Eucharist; we have all the necessary means of growing as human beings and as children of God. It is a mistake to think that a special state of life is the only way of doing it. The persons I know who are most advanced in prayer are married or engaged in active ministries, running around all day to fulfill their duties.

A couple of years ago, I gave a conference to an assembly of lay organizations. These included marriage-encounter and social action groups, secular institutes, and new communities. My talk was based on monastic spirituality, but instead of saying "monastic", I said "Christian". I was amazed to see how most people identified with this traditional teaching. It corresponded to their own experience. This reinforced my conviction that the spiritual journey is for every Christian who takes the Gospel seriously.

Spiritual disciplines, both East and West, are based on the hypothesis that there is something that we can do to enter upon the journey to divine union once we have been touched by the realization that such a state exists. Centering prayer is a discipline designed to reduce the obstacles to contemplative prayer. Its modest packaging appeals to the contemporary attraction for how-to methods. It is a way of bringing the procedures to be found in the contemplative teachings of the spiritual masters of the Christian tradition out of the dusty pages of the past into the broad daylight of the present. The popularity of meditative disciplines from the East is proof enough that some such method is essential today. But centering prayer is not just a method. It is true prayer at the same time. If you are willing to expand the meaning of contemplative prayer to include methods that prepare for it or lead into it, centering prayer can be identified as the first rung on the ladder of contemplative prayer, which rises step by step to union with God.

Centering prayer is a method of refining one's intuitive faculties so that one can enter more easily into contemplative prayer. It is not the only path to contemplation, but it is a good one. As a method, it is a kind of extract of monastic spirituality. It concentrates the essence of monastic practice into two periods of prayer each day. When taking an antibiotic, you have to maintain the right dosage in order to benefit from the medication. You have to keep up the required number of antibodies in the blood stream to overcome the disease. So, too, you have to keep up a certain level of interior silence in the psyche and nervous system if you want to obtain the benefits of contemplative prayer.

Centering prayer as a discipline is designed to withdraw our attention from the ordinary flow of our thoughts. We tend to identify ourselves with that flow. But there is a deeper part of ourselves. This prayer opens our awareness to the spiritual level of our being. This level might be compared to a great river on which our memories, images, feelings, inner experiences, and the awareness of outward things are resting. Many people are so identified with the ordinary flow of their thoughts and feelings that they are not aware of the source from which these mental objects are emerging. Like boats or debris floating along the surface of a river, our thoughts and feelings must be resting on something. They are resting on the inner stream of consciousness, which is our participation in God's being. That level is not immediately evident to ordinary consciousness. Since we are not in immediate contact with that level, we have to do something to develop our awareness of it. It is the level of our being that makes us most human. The values that we find there are more delightful than the values that float along the surface of the psyche. We need to refresh ourselves at this deep level every day. Just as we need exercise, food, rest, and sleep, so also we need moments of interior silence because they bring the deepest kind of refreshment.

Faith is opening and surrendering to God. The spiritual journey does not require going anywhere because God is already with us and in us. It is a question of allowing our ordinary thoughts to recede into the background and to float along the river of consciousness without our noticing them, while we direct our attention toward the river on which they are floating. We are like someone sitting on the bank of a river and watching the boats go by. If we stay on the bank, with our attention on the river rather than on the boats, the capacity to disregard thoughts as they go by will develop, and a deeper kind of attention will emerge.

A thought in the context of this method is any perception that appears on the inner screen of consciousness. This could be an emotion, an image, a memory, a plan, a noise from outside, a feeling of peace, or even a spiritual communication. In other words, anything whatsoever that registers on the inner screen of consciousness is a "thought". The method consists of letting go of every thought during the time of prayer, even the most devout thoughts.

To facilitate letting go, take a relatively comfortable position so that you won't be thinking about your body. Avoid positions that might cut off the circulation because then you will think of your discomfort. Choose a place that is relatively quiet in order not to be disturbed by excessive or unexpected noise. If there is no such place in your household, try to find a quiet time when you are least likely to be disturbed. It is a good idea to close your eyes because you tend to think of what you see. By withdrawing the senses from their ordinary activity, you may reach deep rest. A sudden sound or interruption, like the phone ringing, will shake you up. An alarm clock or timer, which is one way to notify yourself when the time is up, should be a quiet one. If the clock is noisy, stuff it under a pillow. Try to avoid outside noises as much as you can. If noises happen anyway, do not be upset. Getting upset is an emotionally charged thought that is likely to shatter whatever interior silence you may have reached. Choose a time for prayer when you are most awake and alert. Early in the morning before the ordinary business of the day begins is a good time.

Once you have picked a suitable time and place and a chair or a posture that is relatively comfortable, and closed your eyes, choose a sacred word that expresses your intention of opening and surrendering to God and introduce it on the level of your imagination. Do not form it with your lips or vocal chords. Let it be a single word of one or two syllables with which you feel at ease. Gently place it in your awareness each time you recognize you are thinking about some other thought.

The sacred word is not a means of going where you want to go. It only directs your intention toward God and thus fosters a favorable atmosphere for the development of the deeper awareness to which your spiritual nature is attracted. Your purpose is not to suppress all thoughts because that is impossible. You will normally have a thought after half a minute of inner silence unless the action of grace is so powerful that you are absorbed in God. Centering prayer is not a way of turning on the presence of God. Rather, it is a way of saying, "Here I am." The next step is up to God. It is a way of putting yourself at God's disposal; it is He who determines the consequences.

You may be familiar with the gesture of folding your hands together with the fingers pointing upward. This is a symbol of gathering all the faculties together and directing them toward God. The sacred word has exactly the same purpose. It is a pointer, but a mental rather than a material one. The word should be introduced without any force: think it the way you would any thought that might arise spontaneously.

The sacred word, once it is well established, is a way of reducing the ordinary number of casual thoughts and of warding off the more interesting ones that come down the stream of consciousness. It does this not by attacking the thoughts directly but by reaffirming your intention to consent to God's presence and action within. This renewal of the will's consent, as it becomes habitual, creates an atmosphere in which you can more easily disregard the inevitable flow of thoughts.

If you are nervous about doing what may seem like "nothing" for a set period of time, let me remind you that nobody hesitates to go to sleep for six or seven hours every night. But practicing this prayer is not doing nothing. It is a very gentle kind of activity. The will keeps consenting to God by returning to the sacred word, and this is normally enough activity to stay awake and alert.

Twenty to thirty minutes is the minimum amount of time necessary for most people to establish interior silence and to get beyond their superficial thoughts. You may be inclined to remain longer. Experience will teach you what the right time is. At the end of your chosen time span, begin to think your ordinary thoughts again. This may be a good time to converse with God. You may also wish to say some vocal prayer quietly to yourself or to begin planning your day. Give yourself at least two minutes before opening your eyes. Withdrawal from the ordinary use of the exterior and interior senses brings you to a deep spiritual attentiveness, and opening your eyes right away can be jarring.

As your sensitivity to the spiritual dimension of your being develops through the daily practice of this prayer, you may begin to find the awareness of God's presence arising at times in ordinary activity. You may feel called to turn interiorly to God without knowing why. The quality of your spiritual life is developing and enabling you to pick up vibrations from a world you did not previously perceive. Without deliberately thinking of God, you may find that He is often present in the midst of your daily occupations. It is like color added to a black-and-white television screen. The picture remains the same, but it is greatly enhanced by the new dimension of the picture that was not previously perceived. It was present but not transmitted because the proper receptive apparatus was missing.

Contemplative prayer is a way of tuning in to a fuller level of reality that is always present and in which we are invited to participate. Some suitable discipline is required to reduce the obstacles to this expanded awareness. One way is to slow down the speed at which our ordinary thoughts come down the stream of consciousness. If this can be done, space begins to appear between the thoughts, enabling an awareness of the reality upon which they are resting.

In this discussion of centering prayer, I am not exploring methods that help to calm the body, mind and nervous system, such as breathing, yoga, and jogging. Such methods are fine for relaxation, but what we are concerned with is the faith relationship. This relationship is expressed by taking the time to open oneself to God every day, by taking God seriously enough to make a heavy date with Him, so to speak—a date that one would not think of breaking. Since this kind of prayer doesn't require thinking, we can keep our engagement even when we are sick.

The fundamental disposition in centering prayer is opening to God. Christian practice can be summed up by the word *patience*. In the New Testament patience means waiting for God for any length of time, not go-

ing away, and not giving in to boredom or discouragement. It is the disposition of the servant in the Gospel who waited even though the master of
the house delayed his return till well after midnight. When the master finally
came home, he put the servant in charge of his whole household. If you
wait, God will manifest Himself. Of course, you may have a long wait.

I find this practice gets me nowhere. Is it good to try to make the
faculties a blank?

Please don't try to make your faculties a blank. There should always
be a gentle, spiritual activity present, expressed either by thinking the sacred
word or by the simple awareness that you are present to God. The experience of emptiness is the presence of your intention in a very subtle way.
You cannot maintain that experience of emptiness unless your intention
is at work. It may seem like no work because it is so simple. At the same
time, this method of prayer takes time to learn and you need not worry
about experiencing what you may interpret as a blank once in a while. This
prayer is a way of resting in God. If you notice that you have a blank, that's
a thought; merely return to the sacred word.

What do you do when you realize you have been dozing?

If you doze off, don't give it a second thought. A child in the arms
of a parent drops off to sleep occasionally, but the parent isn't disturbed
by that so long as the child is happily resting there and opens its eyes once
in a while.

I was surprised by how fast the time went. Was it really twenty
minutes?

Yes. When the time goes fast, it is a sign that you were not doing much
thinking. I'm not saying it is a sign of good prayer. It is unwise to judge
a prayer period on the basis of your psychological experience. Sometimes
you may be bombarded with thoughts all during the time of prayer; yet
it could be a very useful period of prayer. Your attention might have been
much deeper than it seemed. In any case, you cannot make a valid judgment about how things are going on the basis of a single period of prayer.
Instead, you must look for the fruit in your ordinary daily life, after a month

or two. If you are becoming more patient with others, more at ease with yourself, if you shout less often or less loudly at the children, feel less hurt if the family complains about your cooking—all these are signs that another set of values is beginning to operate in you.

If you have no thoughts at all during centering prayer, you then have no awareness of time. Such an experience reveals the relativity of our sense of time. Our period of prayer, however, will not always seem short. Sometimes it will seem very long. The alternation between tranquility and the struggle with thoughts is part of a process, a refining of the intuitive faculties so that they can be attentive to this deeper level in a more and more stable fashion.

If you're drowsy or very tired, do you have fewer thoughts?

In general, yes, so long as you don't start dreaming! In the monastery we get up at 3:00 A.M., and one is often a little groggy at that hour of the morning. This seems to be part of our particular method, to be so tired that we just can't think. After working hard all day, one may have the same experience in the evening. That can be a help as long as you are alert enough to stay awake and not succumb to the pleasure of drowsing. But don't feel bad if you do fall asleep. You may need a little extra rest.

On the other hand, try to pick a time when you are most likely to be alert so you have a fuller experience of centering prayer rather than nodding your way through it. If you fall asleep, when you awake continue to center for a few minutes so that you don't feel that your prayer was a complete washout for the day. The kind of activity in which you are engaged in this prayer is so simple that it is easy to fall asleep unless you do the modest action that is required, which is to stay alert. Thinking the sacred word is one way of doing this. Jesus said, "Watch and pray." This is what we are doing in centering prayer. Watching is just enough activity to stay alert. Praying is opening to God.

Centering prayer is not so much an exercise of attention as intention. It may take a while to grasp this distinction. You do not attend to any particular thought content. Rather, you *intend* to go to your inmost being, where you believe God dwells. You are opening to Him by pure faith, not by means of concepts or feelings. It is like knocking gently on a door. You are not pounding on the door with your faculties as if to say, "Open in the name of the law! I demand that you let me in!" You can't force this door. It opens from the other side. What you are saying by means of the sacred word is, "Here I am, waiting." It's a waiting game to the *nth* degree. Nothing flashy is going to happen, or, if it does, you should gently return to the sacred word as if nothing had happened. Even if you have a vision or hear infused words, you should return to the sacred word. This is the essence of the method.

> The mood I was in was one of expectation. Then I found myself thinking about the fact that I was expecting something to happen.

Have no expectation in this prayer. It's an exercise of effortlessness, of letting go. To *try* is a thought. That's why I say: "Return to the sacred word as easily as possible"; or, "gently place the sacred word in your awareness." To struggle is to want to achieve something. That is to aim at the future, whereas this method of prayer is designed to bring you into the present. Expectations also refer to the future; hence they, too, are thoughts.

Emptying the mind of its customary routines of thinking is a process that we can only initiate, like taking the stopper out of a bath tub. The water goes down by itself. You don't have to push the water out of the tub. You simply allow it to run out. You are doing something similar in this prayer. Allow your ordinary train of thoughts to flow out of you. Waiting without expectation is sufficient activity.

> What about feelings? Are you supposed to let them go too?

Yes. They are thoughts in the context of this prayer. A perception of any kind whatsoever is a thought. Even the reflection that one isn't having a thought is a thought. Centering prayer is an exercise of letting all perceptions pass by, not by giving them a shove or by getting angry at them, but by letting them go. This enables you gradually to develop a spiritual attentiveness that is peaceful, quiet, and absorbing.

> Is the deeper attention a function of less thought?

Yes. You may even have no thoughts. Then you are at the deepest point that you can go. At that moment there is no sense of time. Time is the measure of things going by. When nothing is going by, there is an experience of timelessness. And it is delightful.

What should we do about external noise?

The best remedy for a sound that you can't control is to let go of your resistance to it and let it happen. External things are not obstacles to prayer. It is just that we think they are. By fully accepting external distractions that you can't do anything about, you may get a breakthrough into the realization that you can be in the middle of all the noise on earth and still experience this deeper attentiveness. Take a positive view of external difficulties. The only thing about which to take a negative view is skipping your daily time for prayer. That's the only no-no. Even if your prayer time seems fraught with noise and you feel like a total failure, just keep doing it.

Is it really possible for people who run around all day to be contemplatives?

Yes. This is not to say that by doing nothing but running around all day people will become contemplatives. On the other hand, you only have to be a human being to be eligible to become a contemplative. It's true that there are certain life styles that are more conducive to the development of a contemplative attitude, but this method works well if you stay with it.

Can you say to people with whom you are traveling, "I'm going to do my meditation now?"

Sure. They might be happy to have a few minutes of quiet themselves.

I am conscious of trying to let thoughts pass, but what happens is that I work with images of my perception of God. They tend to be visual. Is that also a thought that should be discarded?

Any kind of image is a thought in the context of this prayer. Any perception that arises from any one of the senses or from the imagination, memory, or reason is a thought. Hence, whatever the perception may be, let it go. Everything that registers on the stream of consciousness will eventually go by, including the thought of self. It is just a question of allowing every thought to go. Keep your attention on the river rather than on what is passing along its surface.

My way of focusing on God has usually been through an image. If
I remove that image, I have trouble understanding what it is that
I should focus on. Is my attention simply on the word that I am
repeating?

Your attention should not be directed to any particular thought, including the sacred word. The sacred word is only a means of re-establishing
your intention of opening to the true Self and to God, who is at the center
of it. It is not necessary to keep repeating the sacred word. Interior silence
is something that one naturally likes to experience. You don't have to force
anything. By forcing, you introduce another thought, and any thought is
enough to prevent you from going where you want to go.

Some people find it easier to transcend with a visual image rather than
with a word. If you prefer some kind of visual image, choose one that is
general and not detailed; for example, turn your inward gaze toward God
as if you are looking at someone you love.

As you were speaking, it occurred to me that I use images to stop
myself from a free fall.

Some people, when they are quiet, feel themselves on the edge of a
cliff. But don't worry. There is no danger of falling. The imagination is
perplexed by the unknown. It is so used to images, so plugged into them,
that to disengage it from its habitual way of thinking is quite a job. It will
take practice to feel comfortable with this prayer.

CHAPTER FIVE

The Sacred Word as Symbol

The sacred word, whatever one you may choose, is sacred not because of its meaning, but because of its intent. It expresses your intention to open yourself to God, the Ultimate Mystery, who dwells within you. It is a focal point to return to when you notice you are becoming interested in the thoughts that are going by.

Stick to the same word once you feel comfortable with it.[1] If you are moved to choose another word, go ahead and try it, but do not shop around during the same period of prayer. The sacred word is a sign or arrow pointing in the direction you want to take. It is a way of renewing your intention to open yourself to God and to accept Him as He is. While this does not prevent anyone from praying in other forms at other times, the period of centering prayer is not the time to pray specifically for others. By opening yourself to God, you are implicitly praying for everyone past, present, and future. You are embracing the whole of creation. You are accepting all reality, beginning with God and with that part of your own reality of which you may not be generally aware, namely, the spiritual level of your being.

The sacred word enables you to sink into your Source. Human beings were made for boundless happiness and peace, and when we see that we

---

1. Examples of what the sacred word might be: God, Jesus, Spirit, Abba, amen, peace, silence, open, glory, love, presence, trust, etc.

are starting to move in that direction, we don't have to push ourselves. The difficulty is that we are going in the opposite direction most of the time. We tend to identify ourselves with our false self and its concerns and with the world that stimulates and reinforces that false self.

The sacred word is not a vehicle or means to go from the surface of the river to the depths. It is rather a condition for going there. If I hold a ball in my hand and let go, it will fall to the floor; I don't have to throw it.

In similar fashion, the sacred word is a way of letting go of all thoughts. This makes it possible for our spiritual faculties, which are attracted to interior silence, to move spontaneously in that direction. Such a movement does not require effort. It only requires the willingness to let go of our ordinary preoccupations.

Since the will is designed for infinite love and the mind for infinite truth, if there is nothing to stop them, they tend to move in that direction. It is because they are all wrapped up in other directions that their freedom to go where they are naturally inclined is limited. During the time of centering prayer these faculties regain that freedom.

Thus the sacred word is a way of reducing the number of thoughts and of dissolving them into the single thought of opening to God. It is not the means by which we go from a noisy imagination to silence, but a condition that enables us to move into the spiritual realm to which the force of grace is drawing us.

The chief thing that separates us from God is the thought that we are separated from Him. If we get rid of that thought, our troubles will be greatly reduced. We fail to believe that we are always with God and that He is part of every reality. The present moment, every object we see, our inmost nature are all rooted in Him. But we hesitate to believe this until personal experience gives us the confidence to believe in it. This involves the gradual development of intimacy with God. God constantly speaks to us through each other as well as from within. The interior experience of God's presence activates our capacity to perceive Him in everything else—in people, in events, in nature. We may enjoy union with God in any experience of the external senses as well as in prayer.

Contemplative prayer is a way of awakening to the reality in which we are immersed. We rarely think of the air we breathe, yet it is in us and around us all the time. In similar fashion, the presence of God penetrates us, is all around us, is always embracing us. Our awareness, unfortunately, is not awake to that dimension of reality. The purpose of prayer, the sacraments, and spiritual disciplines is to awaken us.

God's presence is available at every moment, but we have a giant obstacle in ourselves—our world view. It needs to be exchanged for the mind of Christ, for His world view. The mind of Christ is ours through faith and baptism, according to Paul, but to take possession of it requires a discipline that develops the sensitivity to hear Christ's invitation: "Behold I stand at the door and knock; if anyone opens I will come in and sup with him and he with me." (Revelations 3:20) It is not a big effort to open a door.

Our ordinary preoccupations involve unconscious value systems. Some thoughts are attractive to us because we have an attachment to them springing from the emotional programming of early childhood. When such thoughts go by, all our lights start flashing because of our heavy emotional investment in the values that they stimulate or threaten. By training ourselves to let go of every thought and thought pattern, we gradually develop freedom from our attachments and compulsions.

In contemplative prayer the Spirit places us in a position where we are at rest and disinclined to fight. By his secret anointings the Spirit heals the wounds of our fragile human nature at a level beyond our psychological perception, just as a person who is anesthetized has no idea of how the operation is going until after it is over. Interior silence is the perfect seed bed for divine love to take root. In the Gospel the Lord speaks about a mustard seed as a symbol of divine love. It is the smallest of all seeds, but it has an enormous capacity for growth. Divine love has the power to grow and to transform us. The purpose of contemplative prayer is to facilitate the process of inner transformation.

It is easier for most people to let go of their thoughts with a word of one or two syllables. But if you find that a visual image is more helpful, use it, provided, of course, that you introduce it on the level of the imagination and return to it whenever you notice you are thinking some other thought. The visual image should be general, not clear and precise. Some people find it especially helpful to pray before the Blessed Sacrament. They usually keep their eyes closed and are simply aware of the presence in which they are praying.

Following one's breathing is another method of quieting the mind. There is a distinction, however, that should be carefully noted. In centering prayer the object is not simply to let go of all thoughts but to deepen our contact with the ground of our being. The intentionality of faith is fundamental. Centering prayer is not just sustained attention to a special word or image or to one's breathing, but the surrender of one's whole being to God. It is not just an experience of our spiritual nature, which can be gained by concentrating on a particular posture, mantra, or mandala. It presupposes a personal relationship; there must be a movement of self-surrender. If, as a Christian, you use some physical or psychological method that is geared to quieting the mind, I suggest that you put it in the context of prayer. For instance, if you follow your exercises as a means of calming your thoughts, do so with the motive of drawing closer to God. Centering prayer is not a relaxation exercise although it may bring relaxation. It is the exercise of our personal relationship with God.

How does the sacred word actually work?

The sacred word is a simple thought that you are thinking at ever deepening levels. That is why you accept it in whatever form it arises within you. The word on your lips is exterior and has no part in this form of prayer; the thought in your imagination is interior; the word as an impulse of your will is more interior still. Only when you pass beyond the word into pure awareness is the process of interiorization complete. That is what Mary of Bethany was doing at the feet of Jesus. She was going beyond the words she was hearing to the Person who was speaking and entering into union with Him. This is what we are doing as we sit in centering prayer interiorizing the sacred word. We are going beyond the sacred word into union with that to which it points—the Ultimate Mystery, the Presence of God beyond any conception that we can form of Him.

The desire to go to God, to open to His presence within us, does not come from our initiative. We do not have to go anywhere to find God because He is already drawing us in every conceivable way into union with Himself. It is rather a question of opening to an action that is already happening in us. To consent to God's presence is His Presence. The sacred word points us beyond our psychic awareness to our Source, the Trinity dwelling in our inmost being. Moreover, God dwells there not as a photograph or statue, but as a dynamic presence. The purpose of this prayer is to get in touch with the activity that God is constantly initiating in our inmost center.

If you keep up this practice every day for several months, you will know whether or not it is right for you. There is no substitute for the experience of doing it. It is like getting to know a new friend; if you meet and converse regularly, you get to know each other faster. That's why we recommend two periods of prayer each day, preferably the first thing in the morning and before supper. Sometimes the "conversation" is engrossing and you experience a certain peace and refreshment. At other times the conversation is like talking about baseball scores when you have no interest in the game; you put up with it because you are interested in a particular person and in whatever interests him or her. An uninspiring period of prayer won't bother you very much if your long-range goal is the cultivation of friendship. The essential discipline is to do it every day.

> What do you do when the entire prayer period consists of wave after wave of thoughts?

When you start to quiet down, you may become aware that your head is full of thoughts coming from both outside and inside. The imagination is a perpetual-motion faculty; it is always grinding out images. So you must expect that on the level of your memory and imagination, thoughts will just keep coming. The main thing is to accept the fact that this is going to happen. No one is going to fall instantly into an ocean of peace where there are no distractions. You have to accept yourself as you are and God as He is, and trust that He will lead you in a way that may not always feel comfortable but that is best for you.

In the case of unwanted thoughts, just let them go without being upset. If you make up your mind that there are going to be a lot of thoughts, you are less likely to get upset when thoughts arrive. If, on the other hand, you feel that the goal of centering prayer is to be free of *all* thoughts, you will be continually disappointed. When you feel disappointed, that is a thought with an emotional charge to it. It shatters whatever interior silence you may have been enjoying.

> Must one say the sacred word constantly?

So long as thoughts are going by of their own accord, you don't have to think the sacred word. In the beginning it is helpful to keep returning to it in order to introduce it into your subconscious and thus to make it easier to recall when you need it during prayer. The basic rule is to let all thoughts on the river go by. As long as they are going by, you don't need to do anything about them. But when you want to look on board one of the boats to see what is hidden in the hold, think the sacred word. Do so gently, however, and without effort.

If you have just had an argument with someone or received bad news, you will need a little preparation for prayer. Reading scripture, walking or jogging around the block, or doing yoga exercises may help to calm your emotional turmoil. One reason to pray early in the day is that events haven't had a chance to upset you yet.

> Does the sacred word disappear permanently or just from time to time during a particular prayer time?

The experience of interior peace is the sacred word at its deepest level. You are experiencing the end of the journey toward which the sacred word is pointing. But this is generally not a permanent state. You keep getting bounced out and have to return again to the sacred word.

> You said that it is not so much repetition of the sacred word that counts but the intention. I was wondering how to hang onto the intention without repeating the word. It seems as if they go together.

In the beginning it is hard to hang on to your intention without continually returning to the sacred word. But this does not mean that you have to keep repeating it. There are forms of Christian prayer similar to mantric practice in the Hindu tradition that consist of repeating the sacred word continuously. This is not the method of centering prayer. In this practice, you only return to the sacred word when you notice you are thinking some other thought. As you become more comfortable with this prayer, you begin to find yourself beyond the word in a place of interior peace. Then you see that there is a level of attention that is beyond the sacred word. The sacred word is a pointer and you have reached that to which it is pointing. Until you have that experience, you must continue to go back to the sacred word in order to reaffirm your intention when you notice you are thinking of something else.

> It seems that a word has a certain emotional quality to it, some kind of atmosphere about it. I was wondering if there was a distinction between trying to stay with the word to see what the feeling quality of that word becomes in centering prayer, and trying to allow everything to drop away, including the feeling quality of that word, in the hope that there is something coming from God's direction.

The meaning of the sacred word or its resonances should not be pursued. It is better to choose a word that does not stir up other associations in your mind or cause you to consider its particular emotional qualities. The sacred word is only a gesture, an expression of your intent; it has no meaning other than your intent. You should choose your word as a simple expression of that intent, not as a source of meaning or emotional attraction. The less the word means to you, the better off you are. It is not a way of going to God or a way into interior silence. Rather, it establishes an interior climate that facilitates the movement of faith. The movement of pure faith is the heart of contemplative prayer. Only God can put content into that kind of faith.

You may reach a point where you no longer think of the sacred word at all. When you sit down for prayer, your whole psyche gathers itself together and melts into God. Interior silence *is* the sacred word at its deepest level. For example, if you take a trip to New York, you buy a ticket at your starting point. But when you get to New York, you don't go to the ticket office to buy another ticket; you are already there. In the same way, use the sacred word to move into interior silence. So long as you experience the undifferentiated, general, and loving presence of God beyond any thought, don't go back to the sacred word. You are already at your destination.

> Sometimes I think that I have reached the tranquillity before I really have. I've tasted the real thing once in a while, but sometimes I think it is there before it really is, and I don't want to go back to the word. Yet I feel that I have to.

Well, don't be too sure. Stay there a few more moments. God is much more intimate and accessible than we think. If the Lord reaches up and pulls you down, great! But since He does not generally do so, there may be something you can do to make it easier for Him. Centering prayer is a method of doing precisely that.

> To what exactly is our attention directed in centering prayer? Is it to the sacred word? To the meaning of the word? To the sound of the word? To a vague sense of God being present?

None of them. We do not try to fix our attention on the sacred word during centering prayer. We do not keep repeating it or think of its meaning. Its sound is of no significance. The sacred word is only a symbol. It is an arrow pointing in the direction intended by our will. It is a gesture or sign of accepting God as He is. Exactly what that is, we don't know. Again, the sacred word is like the needle of a ship's compass pointing out the course in a storm. It is not a means, still less an infallible means, of getting to our destination. It is not within our power to bring about a vague sense of God's being present. What, then, is our principal focus in centering prayer? It is to deepen our relationship with Jesus Christ, the Divine-Human Being.

> In discussions with others who practice centering prayer, I have found that they stop saying the sacred word as soon as some type of silence appears. They stay silent for about five minutes; then thoughts arise and they return to the word. They make another descent into quietness and drop the word; then thoughts arise and they return to it again. What do you think about this dropping and returning, dropping and returning to the word?

Your description sounds as if they know how to do it. Some teachers of prayer are convinced from their experience that contemporary Western minds are so active that they need to repeat a Christian mantra over and over, at least in the beginning. People leading very active lives can certainly benefit from that sort of concentration to hold their attention. The method of centering prayer, however, is not concentrative, but receptive. While both methods are excellent and aim at the same goal, they are not the same and produce different effects in the psyche. In centering prayer, the use of the sacred word is designed to foster the receptive attitude. The interior movement toward God without any word is often enough. You may sink into interior silence as soon as you sit down simply by opening yourself to the presence of God. His presence is already there, but you may not have noticed it because of other duties or occupations.

Contemplative prayer is an incredibly simple kind of attention. It is more intention than attention. As the Spirit gradually takes more and more charge of your prayer, you may move into pure consciousness, which is an intuition into your true Self. There is no way of knowing God directly in this life except by means of pure faith, which is darkness to all the faculties. This darkness is to be understood not as a blanking out of the faculties, but as a transcendence of their activity. Pure faith, according to John of the Cross, is the proximate means of union with God.

Contemplative prayer may open up into various kinds of inner experiences or nonexperiences. In either case, it is a training in being content with God as He is and as He acts. There is tremendous freedom when that disposition is finally established because then you will not look for any form of consolation from God. Spiritual consolations can be as distracting as sensible ones. God gives consolation to heal the emotional problems I was referring to previously. Someone who has been deprived of love needs a lot of affection. The Spirit knows that as well as any psychiatrist. It may be for this reason that the Spirit fills certain people with waves of love and various marks of affection. It doesn't mean that they are holier than others or that the Spirit loves them more. It means that they have more need of love. So he gives them what they need—always, however, with a view to strengthening them so that they may receive more substantial communications, which are beyond the range of psychological awareness.

CHAPTER SIX

The Ordinary Kinds of Thoughts

The great battle in the early stages of contemplative prayer is with thoughts. It is important to recognize the various kinds of thoughts and thought patterns that come down the stream of consciousness and to learn the best way to handle each kind.

The easiest variety of thoughts to recognize is the ordinary wanderings of the imagination. The imagination is a perpetual motion faculty and is constantly grinding away. It is unrealistic to aim at having no thoughts. When we speak of developing interior silence, we are speaking of a relative degree of silence. By interior silence we refer primarily to a state in which we do not become *attached* to the thoughts as they go by.

Suppose you are conversing with someone on the seventh floor of a downtown office building with the windows wide open. There is a constant hum of traffic from the street. Obviously you cannot do anything to prevent the noise from continuing. If you get annoyed and say, "Why don't they keep quiet?" or get in the elevator and go downstairs and start shouting, "Why don't you people shut up?" you will only succeed in bringing your conversation to an end. If you just continue your conversation and put up with the hum, you will gradually develop a capacity to pay no attention to it. This is the best solution for the wanderings of the imagination. Make up your mind that they are going to be present as part of the reality of your inner world. If you fully accept them, they will begin to fade into insignificance.

Once in a while, however, the hubbub gets louder, say at the rush hour, and the decibels increase to an unbearable degree. You have to accept that too. Sometimes you will be persecuted from start to finish by the wanderings and ravings of the imagination. That does not mean that your prayer was no good or that you did not benefit from some degree of interior silence. As you persevere, you will gradually develop new habits and new capacities, one of which is the ability to be conscious of two levels of awareness at the same time. You can be aware of the noise in or around you, and yet you recognize that your attention is grasped by something at a deeper level that is impossible to define but is nonetheless real.

The ability to build a wall around your interior silence during this prayer is a phenomenon that you may experience fairly soon in regard to external sounds. If you fully accept the noise, it scarcely bothers you. If you fight it, struggle with it, or wish it were not there, you will get all wrapped up in particular sounds. Although you may not succeed right away, eventually you will experience a delightful silence at a deep level even though noise is going on around you.

I once visited a family who lived over the Third Avenue El in New York shortly before it was taken down. Their apartment overlooked the tracks. Every now and then a train would roar by. For me the din was absolutely shattering. I thought the train was going right through the living room. But the family seemed to be blissfully unaware of it. They would be chatting away and when a train would come, everybody just stopped talking because it was impossible to be heard. After the train went by, they took up the conversation exactly where they left off as though nothing had happened. They had built the deafening sound into their lives. But for someone who was not used to it, it was not only an interruption but the end of the conversation.

So it is with the rumbling that goes on in our heads. It is so bad sometimes that many people will not put up with it. They say, "Interior silence and contemplative prayer are for the birds. I cannot endure this barrage of tiresome thoughts going through my head." So they get up and leave. If they would just hang on and give themselves a little more time, they would get used to the noise.

The habitual practice of centering prayer gradually reduces the amount of interior noise. In the beginning you are bound to be bombarded by thoughts without end. Most of us, before we begin the method of centering prayer or some other process of quieting the mind, are not even aware of how many thoughts we actually have. But when we start to quiet down, we begin to realize the amazing amount of nonsense stored in our heads. Some people may even get a little scared by how much is going on in there. They find they would rather put up with the ordinary flow of their superficial thoughts.

We should set up conditions that are most conducive for our prayer: find a quiet time of the day away from phones and other foreseeable interruptions. Take the advice of Jesus when he speaks of praying in secret to the Father. If you have a bunch of youngsters running around the house, it may be hard to find a quiet spot or time. For some people the only quiet place may be in the bathtub. In any case, you should find a spot and a time where and when you are least likely to be interrupted. Some noises, like lawn mowers or airplane engines, can be integrated into interior silence, but noises that engage the intellect and imagination, such as loud conversation, are hard to handle.

To sum up, the best response to the ordinary wanderings of the imagination is to ignore them; not, however, with a feeling of annoyance or anxiety, but with one of acceptance and peace. Every response to God, whatever it is, must begin with the full acceptance of reality as it actually is at the moment. Since it is part of our nature to have a wandering imagination, however much you might want to be quiet, accept the fact that thoughts are certain to come. The solution is not to try to make the mind a blank. That is not what interior silence is.

During the entire course of a period of centering prayer, we are slipping in and out of interior silence. One's interior attention is like a balloon on a calm day slowly settling to the ground. Just as it is about to touch the ground, a zephyr comes from nowhere and the balloon starts to go up again. Similarly, in centering prayer there is a tantalizing moment when one feels about to slip into the most delightful silence. That is just the moment that some unwanted thought comes along. It takes great patience to accept the thought and not to be sad because one is prevented from entering that silence. Just start over. This constant starting over with patience, calm, and acceptance trains us for the acceptance of the whole of life. It prepares us for action. There should be a basic acceptance of whatever is actually happening before we decide what to do with it. Our first reflex is to want to change reality or at least to control it.

A second kind of thought that comes down the stream of consciousness during this prayer occurs when, in the course of the wanderings of the imagination, you get interested in some particular thought and notice your attention moving in that direction. You may also feel yourself getting emotionally involved in it.

Any emotionally charged thought or image, whether it comes from outside or from our imagination, initiates an automatic response in the appetitive system. Depending on whether the image is pleasant or unpleasant, you feel a spontaneous like or dislike for it. When you notice that there is curiosity in a particular thought or a clinging sensation, the proper response is to return to the sacred word. This reaffirms your original intention of opening to God and of surrendering to Him.

Our consciousness, as we have said, is like a great river on the surface of which our superficial thoughts and experiences are moving by like boats, debris, water skiers or other things. The river itself is the participation God has given us in His own being. It is that part of us on which all the other faculties rest, but we are ordinarily unaware of it because we are absorbed with what is passing by on the surface of the river.

In centering prayer we begin to shift our attention from the boats and objects on the surface to the river itself, to that which sustains all our faculties and is their source. The river in this analogy has no qualities or characteristics. It is spiritual and limitless because it is a participation in God's being. Suppose you get interested in some boat and find yourself looking in the hold to see what is on board. You are slipping away from your original intention. You must keep turning your attention from what is on the surface of the river to the river itself, from the particular to the general, from forms to the formless, from images to the imageless. Returning to the sacred word is a way of renewing your intention to seek God's inward presence in faith.

Let's return to the image of conversing with a friend on the seventh floor in a downtown office building. At the rush hour horns begin to honk. You start to wonder what is going on, so your attention is drawn away from the conversation with your friend. Courtesy requires that you renew your attention. So you turn your gaze toward your friend as if to say, "Excuse me," or, "As I was saying." In other words, a simple movement to reaffirm your conversation is called for. It is not a question of fighting, stopping or shutting out the noise, but of returning to your original intention. In similar fashion, when, in centering prayer, you notice that you are thinking some other thought, simply give your attention back to God, and as a sign of your intention, think the sacred word.

There is no question of repeating the sacred word as if it were a magic formula to empty the mind or to force the word upon your consciousness. By returning to the sacred word, you reaffirm your choice to converse with God and to be united to Him. This does not demand effort but surrender. Thus whenever you return to the sacred word, do so without exasperation or desperation. Over-reacting is counter-productive. No one cuts a lawn with a bulldozer. All you need to brush away a fly is a movement of your hand. In centering prayer the patient renewal of your intention is sufficient activity.

There are all kinds of ways in which God speaks to us—through our thoughts or any one of our faculties. But keep in mind that God's first language is silence. Prepare yourself for silence in this prayer, and if other things happen, that is His problem, not yours. As soon as you make it your problem, you tend to desire something that is other than God. Pure faith will bring you closer to God than anything else. To be attached to an experience of God is not God; it is a thought. The time of centering prayer is the time to let go of all thoughts, even the best of thoughts. If they are really good, they will come back later.

What do you think of drugs as a means of inducing mystical experience?

Some seem to find spiritual experience through certain psychedelic drugs. It's much more desirable, however, to have a built-in discipline than to depend on drugs, which don't always work as desired. Like certain powerful methods of Eastern meditation, drugs may release material from the unconscious before one is able to deal with it. Some people taking LSD had bad trips because they did not have the psychological preparation to handle what emerged from their unconscious as a result of the drug.

This afternoon I felt very heavy and tired.

You will often notice an alternation between so-called good and bad periods of prayer. Try to give up those categories altogether.

> One thought I had was, "What is the sense of all this? Get up and walk out." Of course, I did not go.

Good. It was just another thought. No matter how much a thought may persecute you, all you have to do is let it go by. By fighting it, you stir up other thoughts.

> I would like to clarify something I was wrestling with. In the past, I have worked determinedly to be centered. I have had a sense of pushing to concentrate versus quietly and gently centering in.

You cannot do this prayer by will power. The more effort you put into it, the less well it goes. When you catch yourself trying hard, relax and let go. Introduce the sacred word gently, incredibly gently, as if you were laying a feather on a piece of absorbent cotton.

Of course, when thoughts are flying at you like baseballs, you look around for some means to protect yourself. But swatting them out of the park is not the way to do it. You should honestly say, "Well, I am being pummeled with these thoughts," and put up with them, remembering that if you just wait, they will all pass by. Do not oppose violence with violence. This prayer is totally nonviolent. A sign of trying too hard is a feeling of tightness in the forehead or in the back of the neck. If you allow your attention to flow with that pain for a few moments, it usually goes away. In other words, accept the fact that you have the pain. Rest in the presence of the pain. Pain has a way of dissolving every other thought. It brings the mind to a single point, which is also the purpose of the sacred word. When the pain subsides, you may need your sacred word again.

> Throughout the first period of prayer there was a counseling session going on down the hall that was loud enough for me to catch bits and snatches. I felt like shouting the sacred word to overcome the noise.

In that situation there is not much you can do but keep returning to the sacred word, yet always with the acceptance of the situation just as it is. Sometimes you cannot do anything but put up with the noise. Think that you are being refreshed at a deeper level, but you just can't enjoy it.

> If at some distant future time, prayer should go beyond thirty minutes, or maybe even an hour, at some point your back may complain. Is that the time to say, "This is where the prayer should cease"? Or should you just keep going?

Your prayer should normally finish before you develop a sore back. One generally has a sense when one's normal period of prayer is over. For some people this might come after twenty minutes. For others, after half an hour or longer. I doubt that you would go for more than an hour without sensing that your prayer was over. But you are free to develop it to that point if you have the attraction and the grace to sustain it.

A better way of prolonging prayer would be set up two periods of ordinary length back to back with a slow, meditative walk around the room for five to ten minutes in between. This would help to dispel the restlessess that may develop from sitting in one position for a long time.

Length of time, however, is not an indicator of the value of one's prayer. The quality of prayer rather than its quantity is what matters. A single moment of divine union is more valuable than a long period of prayer during which you are constantly in and out of interior silence. It only takes a moment for God to enrich you. In that sense the waiting process is a preparation for moments of divine union. Union may occur for only an instant, yet you can be more enriched than someone spending an hour or two on lower forms of contemplative prayer without such a moment of absorption in God. Each of us has to figure out from practice and experimentation when our period of prayer is normally over. To prolong it simply because it is going well is not a good idea.

> As I find myself going deeper, I get frightened and pull myself out of it. I am afraid I am going to stay down there. I do not know if the fear is psychological, physical, or spiritual.

This is a common experience. When you get close to the edge of self-forgetfulness, unless the divine attraction is strong and reassuring, you may experience fear. Our imagination represents the unknown as frightening. If you ignore it and take the plunge anyway, you will find that the water is delightful.

> Last night I let myself go, but then I pulled myself out of it. I was so sorry afterward, and I did not know why I did it.

Before you begin your prayer, say to God, "If You want to pull me over to the other side, go ahead." Then relax. When you submitted to an anesthetic for the first time, you did not know what would happen. If it had not been more or less forced on you, you probably would not have taken it. This prayer is the same sort of situation. You do not know what it is going to be like when you stop reflecting. But try it.

> I was on the verge of a beautiful experience, but that fear was there, so I stopped. I do not know why I pulled myself out of it.

Try not to reflect on the experience at all while it is happening; just let go.

> Is there a way of doing this prayer too frequently so that you lapse into passivity?

Only if you do it for more than five or six hours a day over a long period of time. I do not think three or four hours a day would have any adverse effects at all. Many could pray longer if they built up to it gradually over a period of several months. If you are doing it correctly, you may notice in your activity an increase of energy rather than passivity. That is because you are being freed from a lot of emotional hang-ups that used to exhaust you.

That your superficial faculties are aware of a lot of boats and debris coming down the stream of consciousness does not mean that your other faculties, intellect, and will, are not deeply recollected in God. You may be painfully aware of unwanted thoughts going by and wish they were not there. At the same time you may be aware that something inside of you is absorbed by a mysterious presence that is completely intangible, refined, and delicate. The reason is that your psyche is developing the expanded awareness that I spoke of before, which is able to attend to two planes of reality at the same time, one superficial and the other profound. If you are wrapped up in superficial thoughts or are upset because you have such thoughts, you will not experience the deeper level. There are other times, however, when you will not experience the deeper level, no matter how open you are to it, because of the noise of the imagination or memory.

If the time goes quickly during prayer, that is a sign you were deeply absorbed, perhaps much more than you realized. When there are no objects going by in your imagination, the sense of time is disrupted. If there are no objects going by, there is an experience of timelessness. You are fully aware, yet not of time. Time is a projection of self. When there is no thought, you are free of time. This gives you an intuition into the fact that when the body slips away from the spirit, no great change is going to take place. In deep prayer you do not think about the body anyway. The prospect of dying is not so threatening because you have experienced a preview of what it might be like for the spirit to be separated from the body, and it is delightful.

> During prayer I sometimes have a happy-go-lucky feeling that I find most enjoyable.

You should not take prayer too seriously. There is something playful about God. You only have to look at a penguin or certain other animals to realize that He likes to play little jokes on creatures. The playfulness of God is a profound part of reality. It warns us to not take ourselves too seriously, to realize that God created us with a certain sense of humor.

> Does my guardian angel know what goes on in my centering prayer?

Not unless you tell him! Angels and devils cannot perceive what you are doing in contemplative prayer if it is deep enough. They can only know what is in your imagination and memory, and they can add material to these faculties. But when you are in deep interior silence, what is happening there is God's secret. Only He knows what goes on in the depths of the soul. Some people think that if you quiet the mind, you open yourself up to diabolical forces. But according to John of the Cross, you are never safer than when you are absorbed in God's presence, beyond thoughts and feelings, for there the demons cannot touch you. It is only when you come out of interior silence that they can badger you with temptations. That is why one of the best ways of handling temptations is to slip into the same attitude you take during contemplative prayer. This is what David means when he sings of God in the Psalms as "my refuge, my strength, my rock, my strong fortress, my high tower, my rampart!"[1] We do not have to be afraid of opening ourselves to unknown dangers by practicing contemplative prayer. No one can join us at that level except He who is deeper than that level, the God who dwells within us and out of whose creative love we emerge at every moment.

> During my period of prayer today, there was a thought that kept com-
> ing back. After my prayer was over, it came back again. It was a selfish
> thought. I brought it to the chapel and prayed before the Lord. I made
> a gift of it to Him and then I felt very good. I felt as thought it was
> a splinter getting in my way and I had just taken it out. Is there an
> advantage in taking such things to the Lord in prayer when you can
> talk to Him like that?

By all means follow your attraction. We should go to God with great freedom. I emphasize contemplative prayer because it is an area that has been neglected in recent centuries. The time that you devote to interior silence is not meant to be in conflict with other forms of prayer.

> In the beginning of centering, I used to find it very difficult not to
> break out into vocal prayer if I felt I was not getting somewhere, but
> now I understand that as you try to empty yourself, you make room
> for the Spirit to come in and pray in the innermost recesses of your
> being. This has helped me to put out thoughts. I see there is no need
> for me to try to pray in words, but that I should relax and let Him
> come in to pray.

Prayer is not designed to change God but to change us. The faster we let that happen, the better our prayer is going to be. But once we have got-ten interested in God and have begun to seek Him, the best thing to do is to be silent in prayer and to let Him complete the process. Isn't that the great significance of the Blessed Virgin Mary? She could not possibly forget God. She was prayer in her very being and in every one of her actions.

What is the great thing that Our Lady has done for us? She brought

1. Cf. Psalms 17, 27, 30, 45, 58, 61, 70, 90.

the Word of God into the world, or rather let Him come into the world through her. It is not so much what we do but what we *are* that allows Christ to live in the world. When the presence of God emerges from our inmost being into our faculties, whether we walk down the street or drink a cup of soup, divine life is pouring into the world. The effectiveness of every action depends on the source from which it springs. If it is coming out of the false self, it is severely limited. If it is coming out of a person who is immersed in God, it is extremely effective. The contemplative state, like the vocation of Our Lady, brings Christ into the world.

> I would like to clarify something about using contemplative prayer in times of temptation, stress, or difficulty. I have difficulty with the idea of using prayer to bring me peace. Isn't that a selfish motive?

The principle I had in mind in suggesting slipping into contemplative prayer was to calm your thoughts and feelings, when they are getting hooked on some temptation, by practicing the same kind of letting go that you do during contemplative prayer. Temptation can be treated like any thought that comes down the stream of consciousness. If you let it go by, that is sufficient resistance. If you are unable to do that, you have to exercise other forms of resistance.

> Is the attitude that we develop in our ordinary life-style of letting go of certain things a way of preparing ourselves for prayer in a tangible, practical way, so that it will be easier to let go of the thoughts when we are at prayer?

There is a reciprocal interaction between your activity during the day and your prayer, and vice versa. They mutually support one another.

> How can you pray in deep silence and peace when you are very upset about something?

In such circumstances you cannot hope to pray in silence without some kind of buffer zone. You may have to run around the block, do physical exercises, or some suitable reading. Otherwise, as soon as you sit down and try to be quiet, you will think that you are sitting under Niagara Falls instead of beside the stream of consciousness. You have to give yourself a chance to quiet down before you start to pray. Moreover, some trials are so big that they knock you flat on your face and no matter what means you take to quiet down, you will not be able to settle into interior silence. Giving yourself the usual time to pray, however, will help you to accept the problem and the emotional storm.

Why do you limit the periods of prayer to half an hour in the group?

It seems to be the normal period for prolonged attention. Longer than that might discourage people from starting or continuing. Yet it needs to be long enough to establish the sense of interior silence.

There is a great value in praying at the same time every day and for the same length of time. This will give you a stable reservoir of silence. Dividing the day between two equal periods of deep prayer gives the maximum opportunity for your reservoir of silence to affect the whole day.

The more activity in which you find yourself, the more you will need your times of prayer. Excessive activity has a way of becoming a drain. It also has a mysterious fascination. Like a treadmill or merry-go-round, it is hard to get off. Regular prayer is a real discipline. To interrupt what you are doing in order to pray can be difficult. You need to be convinced that your time of prayer is more important than any other activity apart from some urgent call of charity. You will be surprised that things you have to do fall into place and get accomplished more quickly. You will be able to see the proportionate value of your activities and what should be done first.

Why twice a day and not one longer period?

Twice a day keeps you closer to the reservoir of silence. If you get too far away from the reservoir, it is like being on the end of the water line after everybody has taken what they want from the reservoir. When you turn on the faucet, you only get a few drops. To prevent that from happening, keep the pressure up. You need to keep filling your reservoir until you eventually strike an artesian well. Then the water is always flowing.

Contemplative prayer is a preparation for action, for action that emerges from the inspiration of the Spirit in the silencing of our own agitation, desires and hang-ups. Such silence gives God the maximum opportunity to speak.

During prayer is it all right to reflect on what is happening or is it better to let it go?

During this prayer it is not appropriate to reflect on what is happening. We should completely suspend judgment during this prayer. Afterwards it may be helpful to reflect on it. As you gain experience, you have to keep integrating your prayer into the rest of your life of faith. That requires some form of conceptualization. At the same time, you do not have to analyze your prayer to gain its benefits. It is just as well not to watch what is happening. If you are getting good fruit from it, you will spontaneously notice it. In fact, other people will say, "You do not seem to be as agitated as you used to be." There may be a certain gentleness in you that was not noticed before. You yourself may perceive that, while you used to feel like slugging somebody when you became angry, now you can be satisfied with administering a mild rebuke.

Contemplative prayer fosters a whole different attitude toward one's feelings; it puts them in a different frame of reference. Most extreme feelings come from a sense of insecurity, especially when we feel threatened. But when you are being constantly reaffirmed by the presence of God in deep silence, you are not afraid of being contradicted or imposed upon. You might be humble enough to learn something from insults and humiliations without being overwhelmed by feelings of self-depreciation or revenge. Negative feelings toward oneself tend to be prevalent in our culture due to the low self-image people develop in early childhood, possibly because of our highly competitive society. Anyone who does not win feels that he is no good in this culture, whereas in the quiet of deep prayer, you are a new person, or rather, you are you.

What happens if, because it is consoling, you prolong centering prayer for hours?

If you overdo anything, it is bound to have some bad side effects. Too much joy as well as too much sorrow is fatiguing. The purpose of this prayer is not more prayer or more silence, but the integration of prayer and silence with activity. Consolation of a spiritual kind is so satisfying that it can be a trap. That is why by limiting contemplative prayer to a certain period of time, you have a common sense measure for what is reasonably good for you without running the risk of spiritual gluttony. It is a precious gift to come close to interior silence. Its beauty is so incomparable that it changes one's perception of what beauty is. If you are experiencing this fairly frequently, you gain strength to meet opposition and contradiction. Interior silence is one of the most strengthening and affirming of human experiences. There is nothing more affirming, in fact, than the experience of God's presence. That revelation says as nothing else can, "You are a good person. I created you and I love you." Divine love brings us into being in the fullest sense of the word. It heals the negative feelings we have about ourselves.

> I am afraid that I will stop breathing during the prayer time. I feel most secure when I am getting into my body rhythm. I pay attention to that and am afraid to let it go for too long.

Your breathing may get shallow, but when you need oxygen you will breathe automatically. The body has its own good sense, and if your breathing is getting too shallow, your body will just take a deep breath. It happens in sleep; it will happen in prayer. There is a correlation between thinking and breathing. As the breath gets shallow, thoughts diminish. But as soon as you start thinking, breathing increases too.

> I have heard that if you fast, meditation is enhanced. I guess that it's a matter of training yourself.

The ability to fast is peculiar to each person. What is recommended is that one not do centering on a full stomach. The tendency of this prayer is to reduce the metabolism. A consequence of this is that the bodily processes like digestion slow down. Wait an hour and a half after a full meal. Do not practice just before going to bed. You may experience a surge of energy that might keep you awake for a few hours.

For some, fasting will enhance the experience of centering prayer. It might have the opposite effect on others. If your hunger is so intense that it preoccupies you during the time of prayer, fasting is counterproductive. The principle to follow during centering prayer is to try to forget the body. Simplicity of life, not extremes, fits in better with this kind of practice.

It helps to have the group for moral support. Is it better to center together or alone?

There is moral and psychological support in a group. That's why it is a help to have a support group that meets regularly once a week. On the other hand, some prefer to do it alone because they don't have to adjust to what other people are doing. Both experiences are valuable.

When I find that I am not thinking about anything, I find myself thinking about my breathing.

The best way to handle that is to accept it and to pay no attention. It is as if you were walking down the street to church and someone started to walk beside you. Just keep going, pay no attention to this uninvited companion, and you will wind up where you want to go. Say "yes" to everything that happens. In that way there is a better chance that the obsessive image will go by. A reaction of annoyance or of pleasure intensifies a particular thought.

All thoughts that come down the stream of consciousness are subject to time because they are moving objects, and every object has to go by. If you just wait and do not do anything about them, they will all pass by. But if you try to do something with them or to get away from them, you are stuck with them and you will start going downstream along with them. Then you will have to start over again.

Let thoughts come, let them go. No annoyance, no expectation. This is a very delicate kind of self-denial, but it is more valuable than bodily austerities, which tend to fix one's attention on oneself. Waiting for God without going away, giving the usual time to prayer, and putting up with what goes on in the imagination are the most effective practices for acquiring true devotion. The observance of them will lead to a complete change of heart.

It seems that there are times when you are aware of something around you. The sacred word becomes a reality and you can't make yourself repeat it. This state is not like ordinary waking consciousness, but it doesn't feel like sleep either because there is some plane of awareness.

That is the awareness we're trying to awaken. It might be called spiritual attentiveness. This deep attention is aware of external factors, but they don't make any impression on it because we are captivated by a mysterious inward attention. It's like conversing with someone you love. You may not be saying anything special, but you are wrapped up in that person. If you are eating together in a restaurant, the waitresses may be coming and going, but if you are engaged in an interesting conversation, you don't even notice what they are doing. A waitress can even put down the check and you won't notice that it is the end of the meal or that everyone has left the place and it is time to go. This prayer is not a conversation in words, but an exchange of hearts. It is a higher level of communication than other levels of prayer and tends to integrate these lower levels into itself.

> I found myself dealing with certain kinds of resistance to God. I was half aware of those resistances that I found happening spontaneously. Is it proper to use this period of prayer as a time to wrestle with oneself or God?

When one is inwardly quiet, some of the conflicts that are hidden by the ordinary flow of thoughts begin to come into focus. Normally I would not wrestle with them at this time but would let them go by. The time to reflect on them is after you come out of prayer. The value of contemplative prayer is that it's a total immersion in that aspect of our relationship to God that happens to be the most important—the cultivation of interior silence. Psychological problems may come into focus as a result of periods of great peace, and a breakthrough may emerge. But generally such insights are a trick to get you to think of something. "Anything but silence" is the response of the false self to this kind of prayer. Interior silence goes totally contrary to all the inclinations of the false self. That is why you have to lure it into being still for a little while. However, there may be some special insight into a conflict that you feel inspired to work through right away. Feel free to make an exception. But if it happens too often, you might be making a mistake.

> Today I had an experience of having thoughts come and go without being concerned about them, as I usually am. I am still groping for a balance between using the sacred word and just resting in the presence. There were a few brief moments of simple presence without

my doing anything. Then I would ask myself, should I use the word now?

When you are in deep interior silence, any thought acts on you as tasty bait acts on a fish resting in the deep waters of a lake. If you bite, out you go! Try not to have any expectation. That is not easy. It comes as a result of the habit of letting every thought go by. Eventually you do not care what is coming downstream because it is going by anyway, whether it is pleasurable or painful. I might add that the practice of this prayer will make the events of life easier to handle because you will be able to let them come and go also. Centering prayer is a training in letting go.

CHAPTER SEVEN

The Birth of Spiritual Attentiveness

The chief act of the will is not effort but consent. The secret of getting through the difficulties that arise in contemplative prayer is to accept them. The will is affectivity more than it is effectivity. To try to accomplish things by force of will is to reinforce the false self. This does not dispense us from making appropriate efforts. In the beginning the will is involved in habits that are selfish. We have to make efforts to withdraw from them. But as the will goes up the ladder of interior freedom, its activity becomes more and more one of consent to God's coming, to the inflow of grace. The more God does and the less you do, the better the prayer. In the beginning one is conscious of having to say the sacred word again and again. A better way of expressing that kind of activity is to say that one *returns* to the sacred word or that one gently places the sacred word in one's awareness. The sacred word is the symbol of the subtle spiritual movement of the will. One keeps consenting to God's presence. Since He is already present, one does not have to reach out to grab Him.

The sacred word is the symbol of consenting to God's presence. Eventually the will consents of itself without need of a symbol. The work of the will in prayer is real work, but it is one of receiving. Receiving is one of the most difficult kinds of activity there is. To receive God is the chief work in contemplative prayer.

The method of centering prayer is a way of opening to God at 360

71

degrees. Surrendering oneself to God is a more developed kind of consent. Transformation is completely God's work. We can't do anything to make it happen. We can only prevent it from happening.

As this prayer becomes habitual, a mysterious undifferentiated and peaceful Presence seems to be established inside of you. Some people say they feel that God is living within them. That tranquil Presence that is always there when they settle down becomes their method of prayer.

In the beginning we bring to prayer our false self with its expectations and preconceived ideas. That is why in teaching this prayer I do not speak of effort. The word *effort* is immediately translated in our work ethic into *trying*. Trying dilutes the basic disposition of receptivity that is necessary for the growth of contemplative prayer. Receptivity is not inactivity. It is real activity but not effort in the ordinary sense of the word. If you want to call it effort, keep in mind that it is totally unlike any other kind of effort. It is simply an attitude of waiting for the Ultimate Mystery. You don't know what that is, but as your faith is purified, you don't want to know. Of course, in a sense you are dying to know. But you realize that you can't possibly know by means of any human faculty; so it is useless to expect anything. You don't know and can't know what you are waiting for.

This prayer is thus a journey into the unknown. It is a call to follow Jesus out of all the structures, security blankets, and even spiritual practices that serve as props. They are all left behind insofar as they are part of the false-self system. Humility is the forgetfulness of self. To forget self is the hardest job on earth, but it doesn't come about by trying. Only God can bring our false self to an end. The false self is an illusion. It is our way of conceiving who we are and what the world is. Jesus said, "One who loses his life for my sake will find it." (Matthew 10:39) He also said, "If anyone will come after me let him deny himself [that is, the false self], take up his cross and follow me." (Matthew 16:24) Where is Jesus going? He is going to the cross where even his Divine-Human Self is sacrificed.

For Christians personal union with Christ is the way to come to divine union. The love of God will take care of the rest of the journey. Christian practice aims first at dismantling the false self. It is the work that God seems to require of us as proof of our sincerity. Then He will take our purification in hand, bring our deep-rooted selfishness into clear focus, and invite us to relinquish it. If we agree, He takes it away and replaces it with His own virtues.

At certain stages of human development, there are crisis points; for instance, early adolescence and the period just before young adulthood. Similarly, there is a crisis in spiritual development every time one is called to a higher state of consciousness. When the crisis begins, one hangs on to the false self for dear life. If one resists this path of growth, there is a chance that one might regress to a lower state or play ring-around-the-rosy for a while; there is the possibility of success or failure, of growing or regressing. If one regresses, one strengthens the false self. Then one has to wait until God reissues a new challenge. Fortunately, He has plans for us and does not give up too easily. We see that pattern at work in the way Jesus trained the apostles in the Gospel. He deals with us in similar ways.

The Canaanite woman is a magnificent example of someone undergoing what John of the Cross called the night of sense, the crisis that initiates the movement from dependency on sense and reason to docility to the Spirit. This woman went to Jesus as many other people had done and asked for the cure of her daughter. She didn't expect to have any trouble. She knelt down and made her petition. But Jesus didn't answer her. She prostrated herself, her face in the dust, and still got the cold shoulder. No one was ever treated so roughly by Jesus. As she was grovelling in the dust, he said, "It is not fair to take the children's bread and throw it to the dogs." (Matthew 15:26) The implication is obvious. But she came back with this incredible answer, "You are absolutely right, Lord. But even the dogs eat the crumbs as they fall from their master's table." (Matthew 15:27) Jesus was thrilled. His strange behavior was intended to raise her to the highest level of faith. At the end of the conversation he was able to say to her, "How wonderful is your faith! You can have anything you want!" To get to that place we, too, may have to experience rebuff, silence, and apparent rejection.

Some people complain that God never answers their prayers. Why should He? By not answering our prayers, He is answering our greatest prayer, which is to be transformed. That is what happened to the Canaanite woman.

> Sometimes there are no thoughts. There is only my self-awareness. I don't know whether to let go of it or to be aware of it.

That is a crucial question. If you are aware of no thoughts, you are aware of something and that is a thought. If at that point you can lose the awareness that you are aware of no thoughts, you will move into *pure conscious-*

ness. In that state there is no consciousness of self. When your ordinary faculties come back together again, there may be a sense of peaceful delight, a good sign that you were not asleep. It is important to realize that the place to which we are going is one in which the knower, the knowing, and that which is known are all one. Awareness alone remains. The one who is aware disappears along with whatever was the object of consciousness. This is what divine union is. There is no reflection of self. The experience is tem-porary, but it orients you toward the contemplative state. So long as you *feel* united with God, it cannot be full union. So long as there is a thought, it is not full union. The moment of full union has no thought. You don't know about it until you emerge from it. In the beginning it is so tenuous that you may think you were asleep. It is not like the sense of felt union with the Lord that takes place on the level of self-reflection. Union on the spiritual level is a state of pure consciousness. It is the infusion of love and knowledge together, and while it is going on, it is nonreflective.

There is something in us that wants to *be aware* that we are not aware of ourselves. Even though the willingness to let go of the self is present, we can't do anything to bring it about except by continuing to let go of every thought. If we reflect on self, we start to move out again into the conceptual world.

Divine union for some might seem a bit scary. We can't imagine what such a state of being might be like. We think, "What if I lost conscious-ness? What if I never come back?" If we indulge the fear that we might not come back, we inhibit the process of letting go.

Centering prayer is an exercise in letting go. That is all it is. It lays aside every thought. One touch of divine love enables you to take all the pleasures of the world and throw them in the wastebasket. Reflecting on spiritual communications diminishes them. The *Diamond Sutra* says it all: "Try to develop a mind that does not cling to anything."[1] That includes visions, ecstasies, locutions, spiritual communications, psychic gifts. These are not as valuable as pure consciousness.

It is extremely hard not to reflect on spiritual consolations, especially if you haven't had much experience of them. However, as you approach interior silence and are thrown out enough times, you begin to accept the fact that the grasping method won't work. Don't be discouraged or indulge in guilt feelings. Failure is the path to boundless confidence in God. Always remember that you have a billion chances. This God of ours is not cross-

---

1. Luk, *Ch'an and Zen Teaching*, Series One, p. 173.

ing off anything on our list of opportunities. He keeps approaching us from every possible angle. He lures, draws, nudges, or pushes us, as the case may demand, into the place where He wants us to be.

Eventually you may get used to a certain degree of interior silence. The delightful peace that you may have enjoyed in the early stages of contemplative prayer becomes a normal state. Like anything in life, you can get used to contemplative prayer and not notice the great gifts you are receiving. Habitually you settle down at the beginning of prayer and move into a quiet space, and that's all there is. But that does not mean that you are no longer receiving the prayer of quiet, in which your will is in union with God. If thoughts are going by and you feel no attraction for them, you can be confident that you are in the prayer of quiet. When all the faculties are grasped by God, there is full union. That, however, is not the end of the journey.

What is the relationship of contemplative prayer to the rest of life?

The union established during prayer has to be integrated with the rest of reality. The presence of God should become a kind of fourth dimension to all of life. Our threedimensional world is not the real world because the most important dimension is missing; namely, that from which everything that exists is emerging and returning in each micro-cosmic moment of time. It is like adding a sound track to a silent movie. The picture is the same, but the sound track makes it more alive. The contemplative state is established when contemplative prayer moves from being an experience or series of experiences to an abiding state of consciousness. The contemplative state enables one to rest and act at the same time because one is rooted in the source of both rest and action.

Some people experience a preview of divine union, lose it for a period of time, then have to climb back to it. God can start you off at any point in the spiritual life. If you get a headstart, you have to go back and fill in the gaps. Don't think that some people are lucky because they have visions when they are five or six years old. These people still have to go through the struggle to dismantle the emotional programs of early childhood. These programs are only temporarily put to sleep by the divine action. One great advantage for such persons, however, is that they know by experience what is missing in their lives and that nothing less than God can ever satisfy them. It is a mistake, however, to envy or admire someone else's path. You must be convinced that you have everything you need to reach divine union.

The reason any expectation is a hindrance is that it is a form of clinging, hence a desire to control.

Let go of sensible and spiritual consolation. When you feel the love of God flowing into you, it is a kind of union, but it is a union of which you are aware. Therefore, it is not pure union, not full union. Spiritual consolation is so marvelous that human nature eagerly reaches out for it. We are not about to sit still and pretend it isn't there. We reach out for it with all our being and cry, "If I can only remember how I got here!"

So long as you are moved by such desires, you are still trying to control God. Even if you see the heavens opening and Jesus sitting at the right hand of the Father, forget it. Return to the sacred word. You have nothing to lose. Spiritual communications accomplish their purpose instantly before you have the chance to reflect on them. You have received the full benefit of the gift even if you never think of it again. Letting go of spiritual gifts is the best way to receive them. The more detached you are from them, the more you can receive or rather, the better you can receive. It takes a lot of courage to let go of the most delightful things that can be experienced.

> Why is there such an alternation in prayer between consolation and desolation, interior silence and the bombardment of thoughts, the presence of God and the absence of God?

The alternations in our relationship with God are not unlike the presence or absence of someone we greatly love. In the *Song of Solomon*, God is depicted as pursuing the soul as His beloved. The fathers of the Church had a fondness for this particular verse: "O that his left hand were under my head and that his right hand embraced me."(Song of Solomon 2:6) According to their interpretation, God embraces us with both arms. With the left He humbles and corrects us; with the right He lifts us up and consoles us with the assurance of being loved by Him. If you want to be fully embraced by the Lord, you have to accept both arms: the one that allows suffering for the sake of purification and the one that brings the joy of union. When you feel physical pain or when psychological struggles are persecuting you, you should think that God is hugging you extra tightly. Trials are an expression of His love, not of rejection.

In contemplative prayer, the distress caused by the absence of God is often compensated for by experiences of divine Union. The greater your longing for union with Christ, the more painful it is when he seems to go away. Suffering is part of the warp and woof of living. It is not an end in itself, but part of the price one has to pay for being greatly loved. Love, whether human or divine, makes you vulnerable. The alternation of joy and sorrow in the spiritual journey helps us to be detached from our psychological experiences. True lovers are more interested in being loved for themselves than for their embraces. So it is with God. He wants to be loved for His own sake, for who He is, beyond what we may experience. The tendency to seek the reward of love, which is to be loved in return, is natural. The Spirit teaches us through these alternations to love God as He is in Himself, whatever the psychological content of our experience. That kind of freedom stabilizes the spiritual journey. From then on, the vicissitudes of the journey, while painful at times on the surface, do not disturb the heart that is rooted in divine love.

There is a level in which pain is joy and joy is pain. Then it doesn't matter any more which it is because one is rooted in a place where what matters is divine love. From the point of view of divine love, pain can be joy. It is a way of sacrificing ourselves completely for the sake of the Beloved. It does not cease to be pain, but it has a different quality from ordinary pain. Divine love is the source of that quality. It finds in pain a way of expressing its love with a totality that would not be otherwise possible. Jesus crucified is God's way of expressing the immensity of His love for each of us, proof that He loves us infinitely and unconditionally.

> Can the interior attraction for recollection overtake you during the day in your ordinary occupations?

Yes. I only recommend that when driving a car, you keep your eyes open! Apart from such situations, if one has the leisure, one could give way to it. You also can overdo it. The pleasurable part of prayer is not the goal; it is rather the introduction to it. If you can be united to God without the intermediary of feelings and thoughts, there is no more sense of separation. Spiritual consolation is a means of softening up the faculties and healing them of their various wounds. It gives you a completely different view of God than when you are dealing with Him solely on the basis of good and evil, right and wrong, reward and punishment. As the relationship of intimacy with God begins to deepen, you should not unduly prolong your time of prayer. When there is some duty to be performed, you have to sacrifice for the moment your attraction to interior silence. But if you have nothing urgent going on, I don't see why you can't give in to the attraction for five or ten minutes, or longer, if you have the time.

In contemplative orders there should be great respect for individual expressions of the contemplative life. At different periods of one's development God calls one to more intense community life and at other times to greater solitude. If you are in a community where only one or the other is available, the situation is not conducive to the full expression of the contemplative vocation. Institutions, even the best ones, have limitations. Sometimes God uses confining situations to bring someone to great perfection, but with the general awakening to individual needs in our time, communities will do well to remember that contemplatives have needs, too, and to provide for them in an atmosphere of support and sympathy.

Some of the greatest sufferings of contemplatives have come not from God, but from other people. When Margaret Mary Alacoque was receiving visions of the Sacred Heart of Jesus, she often entered into bodily ecstasy.[2] When the other nuns rose at the signal to leave the choir, she could not get up. Her superiors accused her of disobedience because she was not observing the rule. Some of the sisters thought she must have a devil, and they used to sprinkle her with holy water to protect themselves and the other nuns. You can imagine their faces when they were trying to exorcise the demon out of poor Margaret Mary, who just could not tear herself away from the love of God. Her prayer life was developing in a thoroughly normal way, but her senses could not sustain the strength of the graces that God was giving her. Later, when she became spiritually more mature, her senses did not give way, and then her state of prayer was no longer obvious.

Spiritual consolation that overflows into the senses and into the body is a phase in the growth of contemplative prayer. Some temperaments are more prone to it than others. Some do not experience it at all. If it is especially strong, the body cannot move a muscle and time goes by unnoticed. Centering prayer may give you an inkling of what that might be like. When the period of prayer seems to pass quickly, you can see that if you were just a little deeper, you would have no idea of time at all. If somebody came up and touched you, you would be shaken up. If a community regards such phenomena as dangerous, from the devil, or unlikely to happen to humble religious, then such a community is a poor context for the

2. Poulain, *Graces of Interior Prayer*, Chapter XIV:57.

development of the spiritual life. Unfortunately, such attitudes have been common in religious life for three hundred years because of the prevailing anti-contemplative climate. The fear of false mysticism led to extremes like the Inquisition, which regarded even the writings of Teresa and John of the Cross with suspicion. John of the Cross is now recognized as one of the greatest exponents of the mystical life that the Roman Catholic Church has ever produced. If even he could not escape the suspicion of the Inquisition, what do you think would happen to ordinary religious who were having experiences that they could not articulate because they were not theologians or spiritual directors?

It is one thing to have the grace of interior prayer; another to be able to communicate it. They do not necessarily go together. Sometimes someone who truly has the contemplative experience expresses it in a way that upsets the more conservative element in the environment. Such a person may be labeled a heretic when he is just expressing himself clumsily.

Mystical language is not theological language. It is the language of the bed-chamber, of love, and hence of hyperbole and exaggeration. If a husband says that he adores his wife, it does not mean that he regards her as a goddess. He is just trying to express his *feeling* of love in language that is powerless to do so—except through hyperbole. But if the people in your environment do not understand that kind of language, they may think you are under the influence of the devil.

How does the Charismatic Movement fit in with this contemplative approach to prayer?

The great contribution that the Charismatic Movement has made is to reawaken among contemporary Christians belief in the dynamic activity of the Spirit, who is strengthening, consoling, and guiding us with his unfailing inspiration. Thanks to the Movement, the spontaneity of the early Christian communities described by Paul and by the Acts of the Apostles is being rediscovered in our time. The first believers gathered in communities around the risen Christ to listen to the word of God in scripture, to celebrate in the liturgy, and to be transformed into Christ by the Eucharist. The presence of the Spirit was palpably manifested in these assemblies by means of the charismatic gifts. The gift of tongues seems to have been given to encourage the individual believer; hence, its use in public worship was restricted. Interpretation of tongues, prophecy, healing, teaching, administration, and other gifts provided for the spiritual and material needs of

the various local communities. The continuing work of the Spirit manifested by the development of the Christian contemplative tradition must
now be integrated into this scriptural model revived by the Charismatic
Renewal.

> I know a man who got into the Charismatic Movement, was hav-
> ing profound spiritual experiences, and didn't know what they were.
> His parish priest didn't either. This man was in touch with a con-
> templative nun in a cloistered convent who told him, "Don't worry
> about it; those are typical." She referred him to the appropriate mys-
> tical text and continued to give him instruction.

The Charismatic Movement speaks to the need of Christians today
for a supportive community and for a personal experience of prayer. "Baptism in the Spirit" is probably a transient mystical grace induced by the
fervor of the group or by other factors that we don't know. The gift of tongues
is a rudimentary form of nonconceptual prayer. Since you don't know what
you are saying, you can't be thinking about what you are saying. Those in
the Movement need what that man was fortunate enough to receive, namely, the help and instruction of someone who knew the Christian contemplative tradition. After you have sung the praises of God, shared prayer
together, spoken in tongues, and prophesied for a few years, where do you
go from there? There is a place to go. It is time to introduce periods of silence
into the group, for the members are now fully prepared to move to a more
contemplative expression of prayer. If some silence were introduced into
the meetings, the Movement would hold more people. Groups differ according to their makeup and theological resources, but they all need help
with spiritual teaching. Some Charismatics are opposed to contemplative
prayer because they believe that if you are not thinking, the devil will start
thinking for you. In actual fact, if you are praying in interior silence, the
devil can't get anywhere near you. There is more chance of his suggesting
things to your imagination when you are practicing discursive meditation.
It is only when you come out of interior silence and reemerge into the world
of the senses and reasoning that he can put his finger in the pie and stir
things up. The Charismatic Movement has great potential. To fulfill its
promise, however, it needs to be open to the Christian contemplative
tradition.

CHAPTER EIGHT

The More Subtle Kinds of Thoughts

The first kind of thought that regularly comes down the stream of consciousness when one begins to practice centering prayer is woolgathering. This may consist of things that we were doing or thinking about prior to our time of prayer. Or again, an outside sound, a vivid memory, or some plan for the future may attract and capture our attention. In the simile we have been using, these thoughts are like boats floating down the stream of consciousness. Our normal, habitual reaction is to say, "What is this? I wonder what is in the hold?" Instead, gently return to the sacred word, moving from the particular thought to the general loving attention to God that that word reaffirms. And let the boat go by. When another boat comes down, let it go by. If a whole fleet comes down, let them all go by.

At first this is bothersome because you want to remain quiet. Little by little you begin to develop two attentions at once. You are aware of the superficial thoughts. At the same time you are aware of an undifferentiated presence that mysteriously attracts you. It is a deeper attention, a spiritual attentiveness. You are aware of both levels of attention going on at once. To develop that deeper attention is more important than worrying about the superficial thoughts. They will cease to attract you after a while.

A second kind of thought that comes down the stream of consciousness might be compared to a flashy boat that captures your attention and makes you feel like climbing aboard. If you give in to the inclination and hop on board, you start heading downstream. You have identified yourself in some degree with the thought. To return to the sacred word is to reaffirm your original intention of opening to the divine presence. The sacred word is a means of liberating yourself from the tendency to get stuck on an attractive thought. If you are hooked or about to be hooked, let go promptly but with a very gentle interior movement. Any form of resisting thoughts is itself a thought. Moreover, it is a thought with an emotional charge to it. Emotionally charged thoughts hinder the basic disposition you are engaged in cultivating, waiting upon God in the mystery of His Presence. So let go of all thoughts, and when tempted to pursue one of them, return to the sacred word. Do it as gently as if your attention were a drop of dew descending on a blade of grass. If you allow yourself to be annoyed at being pulled out of the silent waters that you were enjoying, you will just go farther downstream.

When you begin to quiet down and enjoy a certain peace, you don't want to think of anything. You just want to be quiet. Then another kind of thought emerges. It could be some bright light about the spiritual journey or some great psychological insight into your past life. Or you have a problem with a member of your family and suddenly see how it can be resolved. Or you discover the perfect argument for converting your friends. Of course, when you come out of prayer, you see that your brilliant ideas were utterly ridiculous. They looked wonderful in the darkness of the deep waters of silence, but in the light of day you realize that they were bait to lure you out of interior peace and quiet.

Again, you may feel an overwhelming urge to pray for someone. It is important to pray for others, but this is not the time to do it. Any effort you make at this point is counterproductive. This is God's opportunity to talk to you. It would be like interrupting someone who wants to confide something to you. You know how it is when you are trying to tell a friend something important and he keeps interrupting you with ideas of his own. In this prayer you are listening to God, listening to His silence. Your only activity is the attention that you offer to God either implicitly by letting go of all thoughts or explicitly by returning to the sacred word.

Preachers and theologians who are trying to practice contemplative prayer have a special problem with good thoughts. Just when they are quiet, they get some incredible inspiration. A theological problem they have been trying to fathom for years suddenly becomes as clear as crystal. There is a tendency for them to think, "I must reflect about this for just a second so I won't forget it after my prayer is over." That is the end of their interior silence. When they come out of prayer, they can't even remember what the bright idea was. When one is in deep quiet, one is very susceptible to brilliant intellectual lights. Most of the time they are just illusions. Human nature does not like to be empty before God. If you are making headway in this prayer, you will be tempted by the jealous demons who see that you are getting some place and try to trip you up. To hinder your progress they dangle various kinds of tasty bait in front of your imagination. Like a little fish enjoying deep waters, you feel engulfed by God on all sides when suddenly this bait is lowered into your peaceful space. You bite on it and out you go.

It may be hard to convince yourself of the value of interior silence. But if you are going to practice centering prayer, the only way to do it is to ignore every thought. Let it be a time of interior silence and nothing else. If God wants to speak to you in successive words, let Him do so during the other twenty three hours of the day. He will be more pleased that you preferred to listen to His silence. In this prayer God is speaking not to your ears, to your emotions, or to your head, but to your spirit, to your inmost being. There is no human apparatus to understand that language or to hear it. A kind of anointing takes place. The fruits of that anointing will appear later in ways that are indirect: in your calmness, in your peace, in your willingness to surrender to God in everything that happens. That is why interior silence is greater than any insight. It also saves you a lot of trouble. Pure faith is the surest and straightest road to God. Human nature wants to recall spiritual experiences of one kind or another in order to be able to explain them to oneself and to others. The remembrance of spiritual experiences is okay up to a point, but such experiences are not as important as interior silence. Don't reflect on them during prayer. If they have genuine value, they will come back to you later. The deeper your interior silence, the more profoundly God will work in you without your knowing it. Pure faith consents and surrenders to the Ultimate Mystery just as He is; not as you think He is or as someone has told you He is, but as He is in Himself.

There is no greater way in which God can communicate with us than on the level of pure faith. This level does not register directly on our psychic faculties because it is too deep. God is incomprehensible to our faculties. We cannot name Him in a way that is adequate. We cannot know Him with our mind; we can only know Him with our love. That is what some

mystical writers call *unknowing*. It is by *not* knowing Him in the ways that
we now know Him, that we *do* know Him. Visions, locutions or ecstasies
are like frosting on a cake. The substance of the journey is pure faith.

A special kind of thought occurs when our ordinary psychic self is quiet.
If you have ever made wine, you know that after the new wine has been
separated from the dregs, it is poured into a barrel and what is called a finer
is introduced. A finer is a liquid that forms a thin film throughout the barrel
and gradually sinks to the bottom in the course of two or three months,
carrying with it all the foreign bodies in the wine. What is happening to
your psyche in contemplative prayer is quite similar. The sacred word is
the finer and the silence to which it inclines you is the process that clarifies
your consciousness. As your consciousness is clarified, you resonate with
spiritual values and the radiance of God's presence.

There is an immediacy of awareness in contemplative prayer. It is a
path to the rediscovery of the simplicity of childhood. As an infant becomes aware of its surroundings, it is not so much *what* it sees that delights
it as it is the *act* of seeing. I once heard about a little girl of wealthy par-
ents who loved to play with her mother's jewelry. When her mother wasn't
around and the nurse couldn't capture her in time, she used to gather her
mother's diamonds and throw them into the toilet bowl. She loved to hear
the splash as she watched the beautiful diamonds sinking in the water. As
she grew older, she learned to flush the toilet. The members of the household were tearing their hair. How were they to cure the dear child of this
terrible habit? The little girl had no interest in the value of the jewelry.
Her mother, of course, thought they had great value. The little girl simply
enjoyed the immediacy of the experience, the sparkling diamonds splashing
into the water. She had the freedom and joy of true detachment.

As we grow older, it is important to develop our analytical judgment,
but we shouldn't lose the enjoyment of reality as it is, the value of *just being* and of *just doing*. In the Gospel, Jesus invites us to become like little
children, to imitate their innocence, confidence, and direct contact with
reality. He doesn't invite us, of course, to imitate their childishness, and
their tantrums. If our value system doesn't allow us to enjoy anything without putting a price on it, we miss a great part of the beauty of life. When
we bring this value system into the domain of prayer, we can never enjoy
God. As soon as we start enjoying Him, we have to reflect, "Oh boy, I'm
enjoying God!" And as soon as we do that, we are taking a photograph
of the experience. Every reflection is like a photograph of reality. It isn't

our original experience; it is a commentary on it. Just as a picture only approximates reality, so every reflection is one step back from experience as it actually is. When we experience the presence of God, if we can just not *think* about it, we can rest in it for a long time. Unfortunately, we are like starving people when it comes to spiritual things, and we hang on to spiritual consolation for dear life. It is precisely that possessive attitude that prevents us from enjoying the simplicity and childlike delight of the experience.

In contemplative prayer we should ignore our psychological experiences as much as we can and just let them happen. If you are at peace, wonderful; don't think about it. Just be at peace and enjoy it without reflecting. The deeper the experience you have of God, the less you will usually be able to say about it. When you try to conceptualize, you are using your imagination, memory, and reason—all of which bear no proportion to the depth and immediacy of divine union. A childlike attitude makes sense in this situation. You don't have to *do* anything. Just rest in God's arms. It is an exercise of *being* rather than of *doing*. You will be able to accomplish what you have to do with much greater effectiveness and joy. Much of the time we run on cylinders that are out of oil or a bit rusty. Our powers of giving are pretty well used up by noon on most days. Contemplative prayer opens you to the power of the Spirit. Your capacity to keep giving all day long will increase. You will be able to adjust to difficult circumstances and even to live with impossible situations.

The third kind of thought, if consented to prevents you from entering into your own deep space. That is why no matter how glamorous the thought or how many problems it seems to solve, you should forget it. You can always think about bright ideas later in the day, and then it may be fruitful to do so. In this prayer we are cultivating purity of motivation. In the Christian path, motivation is everything. When there are no obstacles in ourselves to receiving the light, the light that is always shining will shine in us. As long as we are under the influence of the false self and its ego trips, we have the shades drawn. Unfortunately, the false self doesn't just drop dead upon request. We can't just say, "That's the end of it," and expect it to disappear. The false self is extremely subtle. Without God's special help, we could never escape from it. In addition, the trials that come our way would flatten us.

The attitude that reinforces the false self more than anything else is our instinct to possess something, including our own thoughts and feelings. This instinct has to be relinquished. Most of us are starved for spiritual experience. When it begins to happen, everything in us reaches out for it. We can't help ourselves at first. As we learn through bitter experience that grasping for spiritual experience gets us thrown out on the bank, it dawns on us that this is not the way to proceed. If we can let go of our clinging attitude toward this deep peace, we will move into a refined joy and an inner freedom where spiritual experience no longer looms so large. We can have all we want of divine consolation if we don't try to possess it. As soon as we want to possess it, it is gone. We have to accept God as He is, without trying to possess Him. Whatever we experience of Him must be allowed to pass by like every other thought that comes down our stream of consciousness. Once we know that our destination lies beyond any kind of spiritual experience, we realize that it is useless to hang on to anything along the way. Then we won't settle down under a palm tree in some oasis along the route. An oasis is refreshing, but it is not the purpose of the journey. If we keep going, even if we are only stumbling or crawling along, we will come to the interior freedom that is the ripe fruit of docility to the Spirit.

The third kind of thought occurs when we enter into deep peace, and the inclination to reach out for bright ideas lures us out of the quiet depths. The sacred word is not a mantra in the strict sense of the word. We do not keep saying it until we drill it into our unconscious. It is rather a condition, an atmosphere that we set up, that allows us to surrender to the attractive force of the divine Presence within us. Spiritual consolation is a radiance of that Presence. It is not the Presence of God as such. In this life we cannot know God directly and still live. To know Him directly is what the next life is all about. The closest way to know Him in this life is by pure faith, which is beyond thinking, feeling, and self-reflection. Pure faith is experienced best when there is no psychological experience of God. God is beyond sensible or conceptual experience. The state of pure faith is beyond anything we can imagine. We simply look around and realize that the divine Presence is everywhere. It just *is*. We have opened ourselves wide enough to be *aware* of what is without being able to *say* what it is.

The fourth kind of thought also takes place when we are in deep, all-encompassing peace, empty of thoughts and images. A mysterious fullness, a kind of luminous darkness, seems to surround us and penetrate our consciousness. We enjoy deep calm even though we are dimly aware of the ordinary flow of unwanted thoughts. They are especially distressing at such a time because we know if we get hooked on one of them, we are going to be carried out of that peace. We don't even want to return to the sacred word. We don't want to do anything except allow ourselves to be bathed in the light and love that seem to be tenderly anointing our inmost being. It is as if God planted a great big kiss in the middle of our spirit and all the wounds, doubts, and guilt feelings were all healed at the same moment. The experience of being loved by the Ultimate Mystery banishes every fear. It convinces us that all the mistakes we have made and all the sins we have committed are completely forgiven and forgotten.

Meanwhile, into that silence, into that state of no-thinking, no-reflection, and ineffable peace, comes the thought: "At last, I'm getting somewhere!" Or, "This peace is just great!" Or, "If only I could take a moment to remember how I got into this space so that tomorrow I can return to it without delay." Out you go, as fast as lightning, right onto the bank. And then you say, "Oh, God! What did I do wrong?"

How do you let God act in this prayer?

It's difficult to let God act under all circumstances. Letting go and not reflecting on what you are doing is the correct way to conduct yourself in this prayer. The method doesn't consist in how you sit or in the length of time you give, but in how you handle the thoughts that arise. I think it can be said that the essential point of all the great spiritual disciplines that the world religions have evolved is the letting go of thoughts. Everything else is subsidiary to that. The goal is to integrate and unify the various levels of one's being and to surrender that integrated and unified being to God.

Are you ever aware of God during contemplative prayer, or is it only afterwards that you can know that God was there? How is it possible to be aware of something and not reflect on it?

You can be aware of the undifferentiated presence of God and not have any explicit reflection about it. Pure awareness is the immediacy of experience. Our training and education have programmed us for reflection. But one can be so absorbed in an experience that one does not reflect. Have you ever enjoyed something so much that you didn't have time to think of what you were enjoying?

Yes, but I guess you would feel the enjoyment.

Of course. Just don't reflect on the feeling. If you do, you reduce the experience to something that you can understand, and God isn't something you can understand. The awareness of God is shot through with awe, reverence, love, and delight all at once.

We are made for happiness and there is nothing wrong in reaching out for it. Unfortunately, most of us are so deprived of happiness that as soon as it comes along, we reach out for it with all our strength and try to hang on to it for dear life. That is the mistake. The best way to receive it is to give it away. If you give everything back to God, you will always be empty, and when you are empty, there is more room for God.

The experience of God usually comes as something you feel you have experienced before. God is so well suited to us that any experience of Him is a feeling of completion or well-being. What was lacking in us seems to be somehow mysteriously restored. This experience awakens confidence, peace, joy, and reverence all at the same time. Of course, the next thing that occurs to us is: "This is great! How am I going to hang on to it?" That's the normal human reaction. But experience teaches that that is exactly the worst thing to do. The innate tendency to hang on, to possess, is the biggest obstacle to union with God. The reason we are possessive is that we feel separated from God. The feeling of separation is our ordinary psychological experience of the human condition. This misapprehension is the cause of our efforts to look for happiness down every path that we can possibly envision when actually it is right under our noses. We just don't know how to perceive it. Since the security that we should have as beings united with God is missing, we reach out to bolster up our fragile self-image with whatever possessions or power symbols we can lay hold of. In returning to God, we take the reverse path, which is to let go of all that we want to possess. Since nothing is more desirable or delightful than the feeling of God's presence, that, too, has to be a thought we are willing to let go of.

Trying to hang on to God's presence is like trying to hang on to the air. You can't carve out a piece of it and hide it in your top bureau drawer. Similarly, you can't carve out a piece of the presence of God and hide it in the closet or store it in the refrigerator until the next period of prayer. This prayer is an exercise in letting go of everything. As it develops, it will help you to let go of things and events that arise outside the time of prayer. This doesn't mean that you do not use the good things of this world. It is only the clinging or addiction to things that reduces the free flow of God's grace and that hinders the enjoyment of His Presence.

Do thoughts always keep coming? It seems like I'm able to maintain a feeling of peace for a time. Then all of a sudden the thoughts roll in again. Is that always the way it happens?

To be in and out of peace is normal in every period of prayer, although there might be some periods that are uniformly quiet throughout. But in that case you are likely to find that the next time you pray, you will be filled with what airline pilots call turbulence, and you will be bounced around quite a bit by persistent and disturbing thoughts. This is not a disaster but something one has to accept. The alternation between peace and thought-barrage is an important part of the process. They are two sides of the same coin.

Please keep in mind that the method of centering is only one form of prayer and doesn't exclude other forms of prayer at other times. It is like Jacob's ladder in the Old Testament. After his vision of the Lord in the form of an angel who wrestled with him all night, Jacob fell asleep. He saw a ladder reaching from earth to heaven with angels descending and ascending. The ladder represents different levels of consciousness or of faith. We should communicate with God on every level of our being: with our lips, our bodies, our imaginations, our emotions, our minds, our intuitive faculties, and our silence. Centering prayer is only one rung of the ladder. It is a way of giving God a chance to speak to us. While our spontaneous chats with God are good, there is a level that is even better. As in human friendship, there is a conversational level. But as friendship grows more intimate, the level of communion develops, where the two can sit together and say nothing. If they say nothing, does that mean they are not finding deep enjoyment in the relationship? There are obviously different ways and different levels of expressing one's relationship with another person and with God. God clearly deals with us in a personal way. This prayer adds a dimension to one's relationship with God that is more intimate than the other levels. There is nothing wrong with vocal prayer, but it isn't the only way or the most profound way of praying.

Could it be that the one who practices contemplative prayer for long stretches of time every day might develop some form of illness?

If you had a lot of time for prayer and were in a particularly consoling period in your development, prayer could be so delightful that you might try to prolong it as much as possible. But to be consoled is not the object of contemplative prayer. Teresa of Avila made fun of certain nuns in her convents who practiced so much of this kind of prayer that they became sick. The reason was that by remaining in interior silence for seven or eight hours a day, and perhaps longer, their senses became so withdrawn from their ordinary occupations that they probably experienced what we call today sensory deprivation. When we spend a great deal of time in interior silence, the metabolism goes down, which means that less blood is going to the brain. This is fine for a limited period of time such as during a retreat, but if you keep it up day after day, you may get spaced-out. If you continue this practice for more than a week, you need supervision. Everything has to be done with discretion. Generally people overdo discretion on the side of making sure they do nothing that might injure their health. But there are some people who do the opposite, and they may need to be restrained.

> Is there any value in prolonging the time of contemplative prayer?

To do it more than twice a day may hasten the process of self-knowledge. As a result, you may get insights into things from your past that you have not previously faced or handled. It is characteristic of the human condition to avoid seeing our own hang-ups. The development of contemplative prayer from this point of view is a process of liberation from everything that prevents us from being completely honest with ourselves. The more confidence you have in God, the more you can face the truth about yourself. You can only face up to who you really are in the presence of someone you trust. If you trust God, you know that no matter what you have done or not done, He is going to go on loving you. As a matter of fact, He always knew the dark side of your character and He is now letting you in on the secret like a friend confiding to a friend. Insights of self-knowledge, instead of upsetting you, bring a sense of freedom. They lead you to the point where you can ask yourself, "Why think of myself at all?" Then you have the freedom to think how wonderful God is and you care little what happens to you.

> It seems paradoxical that at some point during the prayer you become aware of the fact that you are not thinking at all. What do you do with that?

If you are actually not thinking, there is not even the thought that you are not thinking. There is just pure awareness, and that is the proximate goal of contemplative prayer. The ultimate goal, of course, is to integrate your whole being with its active and passive, masculine and feminine, expressing and receptive aspects. If you begin to be aware of the fact that you are not thinking at all and can just not think that thought, you have it made. There is only a short step from that point to divine union. Of course, you eventually will be thrown out of that delicious silence and your mind will start wandering again. As soon as you notice that you are coming out of interior silence, go back with the gentlest kind of attention to the Presence. The thought of not having a thought is the last preserve of self-reflection. If you can get beyond self-reflection, allow yourself to be self-forgetful, and let go of the compulsion to keep track of where you are, you will move into deeper peace and freedom. There is a conviction deep inside of us that if we ever stop reflecting on ourselves, we will disintegrate or suffer some similar fate. That is not true. If we ever stop reflecting on ourselves, we will move into perfect peace.

> I know when to use the sacred word, but I do not know when *not* to use it.

There is a state of no-thinking and that is where we want to go. It is elusive because of our inveterate tendency to reflect. This innate tendency to be aware of oneself is the last stronghold of self-centeredness. Anthony of Egypt is noted for this famous saying: "Perfect prayer is not to know that you are praying." What I have just described is the state of mind that Anthony is talking about. When you are in perfect prayer, the Spirit is praying in you. The surrender of the false self to God is death to the false self. This is the experience that Jesus was trying to explain to Nicodemus when he said, "You have to be reborn." (John 3:3) One has to die before one can be reborn. Nicodemus replied, "How can someone go back into the womb?" Jesus continued, "You do not understand what I am talking about. I am talking about the Spirit and I am speaking spiritually. The wind blows where it will, and you do not know where it is coming from or where it is going. So it is with everyone who is born of the Spirit." In other words, to be moved by the Spirit is an entirely new way of being in the world.

> I have been using the prayer of centering for over a year, but I have clung to the sacred word like a drowning man clinging to a tire. At

one of the prayer periods today, the tire was getting in my way, so I threw it away. I thought that maybe that was a step forward.

By all means, throw away your life preserver. It's preserving the wrong life. The false self must die if you are to be reborn and live by the Spirit.

As a person becomes more advanced in prayer, will he or she have more need of spiritual direction?

There are times when spiritual direction can be very helpful by way of encouragement and support. In contemplative prayer, every now and then you run into heavy weather. As you go deeper into the unconscious through interior silence, you may hit something like an oil well and up will come a whole stream of stuff. You may have a period of several months or years when it is rough going. These are the periods that John of the Cross calls "dark nights." In such situations, one needs reassurance. For some people, these periods of trial are tougher than they are for others. They need reassurance, and then a spiritual director can be a great help. But if the director does not have experience of this kind of prayer, he or she can do more harm than good.

Sometimes all you need is to wait and not lose heart. When that oil well runs dry, you will move to a new depth. Or again, it is like being in an elevator that gets stuck between floors. You just have to wait until whatever it is that is an obstacle has been removed.

A spiritual director should be someone who has enough experience to be able to perceive with some degree of certitude where you are on the spiritual path. A director can usually discern this from the kind of life that people are leading. If they are obviously seeking God but are having problems that make them think that they are the worst sinners that ever existed, the director has to know how to say, "Forget it! You are the luckiest person on earth!" When you are in the dark night of purification, you are a very poor judge of your own case. One of the trials you have to expect is being unable to find anyone who can help you. God may arrange it that way so that you have to put all your trust in Him.

CHAPTER NINE

The Unloading of the Unconscious

A fifth kind of thought arises from the fact that through the regular practice of contemplative prayer the dynamism of interior purification is set in motion. This dynamism is a kind of divine psychotherapy, organically designed for each of us, to empty out our unconscious and free us from the obstacles to the free flow of grace in our minds, emotions, and bodies.

Empirical evidence seems to be growing that the consequences of traumatic emotional experiences from earliest childhood are stored in our bodies and nervous systems in the form of tension, anxiety, and various defense mechanisms. Ordinary rest and sleep do not get rid of them. But in interior silence and the profound rest that this brings to the whole organism, these emotional blocks begin to soften up and the natural capacity of the human organism to throw off things that are harmful starts to evacuate them. The psyche as well as the body has its way of evacuating material that is harmful to its health. The emotional junk in our unconscious emerges during prayer in the form of thoughts that have a certain urgency, energy, and emotional charge to them. You don't usually know from what particular source or sources they are coming. There is ordinarily just a jumble of thoughts and a vague or acute sense of uneasiness. Simply putting up with them and not fighting them is the best way to release them.

As the deep peace flowing from contemplative prayer releases our emotional blocks, insights into the dark side of our personality emerge and multiply. We blissfully imagine that we do good to our families, friends, and business or professional associates for the best of reasons, but when this dynamism begins to operate in us, our so-called good intentions look like a pile of dirty dishrags. We perceive that we are not as generous as we had believed. This happens because the divine light is shining brighter in our hearts. Divine love, by its very nature, accuses us of our innate selfishness.

Suppose we were in a dimly lit room. The place might look fairly clean. But install a hundred bulbs of a thousand watts each, and put the whole room under a magnifying glass. The place would begin to crawl with all kind of strange and wonderful little creatures. It would be all you could do to stay there. So it is with our interior. When God turns up the voltage, our motivation begins to take on a wholly different character, and we reach out with great sincerity for the mercy of God and for His forgiveness. That is why trust in God is so important. Without trust we are likely to run away or say, "There must be some better way of going to God."

Self-knowledge in the Christian ascetical tradition is insight into our hidden motivation, into emotional needs and demands that are percolating inside of us and influencing our thinking, feeling, and activity without our being fully aware of them. To give an example: When I was an abbot, which is a father image in a monastery, I was struck by the fact that some of the younger members of the community were unconsciously treating me as their real father. I could see that they were working out emotional hassles with authority figures from their early childhood. They were not relating to me as me. When you withdraw from your ordinary flow of superficial thoughts on a regular daily basis, you get a sharper perspective on your motivation, and you begin to see that the value systems by which you have always lived have their roots in prerational attitudes that have never been honestly and fully confronted. We all have neurotic tendencies. When you practice contemplative prayer on a regular basis, your natural resources for psychic health begin to revive and you see the false value systems that are damaging your life. The emotional programs of early childhood that are buried in your unconscious begin to emerge into clear and stark awareness.

If in your psyche there are obstacles to opening yourself to God, divine love begins to show you what these are. If you let go of them, you will gradually unfold in the presence of God and enjoy His Presence. The inner dynamism of contemplative prayer leads naturally to the transformation of your whole personality. Its purpose is not limited to your moral improvement. It brings about a change in your way of perceiving and responding to reality. This process involves a structural change of consciousness.

As you experience the reassurance that comes from interior peace, you have more courage to face the dark side of your personality and to accept yourself as you are. Every human being has the incredible potential to become divine, but at the same time each of us has to contend with the historical evolution of our nature from lower forms of consciousness. There is a tendency in human nature to reach out for more life, more happiness, more of God; but there are also self-destructive tendencies that want to go back to the unconscious and instinctual behavior of the beasts. Even though we know that there is no happiness in such regression, that aspect of the human condition is always lurking within us. Archbishop Fulton Sheen used to say, "Barbarism is not behind us but beneath us." In other words, violence and the other instinctual drives remain as seeds that can develop, if unchecked, into all kinds of evil.

We have to come to grips with these tendencies in order for the fullness of grace to flow through us. Contemplative prayer fosters the healing of these wounds. In psychoanalysis the patient relives traumatic experiences of the past and in doing so, integrates them into a healthy pattern of life. If you are faithful to the daily practice of contemplative prayer, these psychic wounds will be healed without your being retraumatized. After you have been doing this prayer for some months, you will experience the emergence of certain forceful and emotionally charged thoughts. They don't normally reveal some traumatic experience in early life or some unresolved problem in your present life. They simply emerge as thoughts that arise with a certain force or that put you in a depressed mood for a few hours or days. Such thoughts are of great value from the perspective of human growth even though you may feel persecuted by them during the whole time of prayer.

When the unloading of the unconscious begins in earnest, many people feel that they are going backwards, that contemplative prayer is just impossible for them because all they experience when they start to pray is an unending flow of distractions. Actually, there are no distractions in contemplative prayer unless you really want to be distracted or if you get up and leave. Hence, it doesn't matter how many thoughts you have. Their number and nature have no effect whatever on the genuineness of your prayer. If your prayer were on the level of thinking, thoughts that were extraneous to your reflections would indeed be distracting. But contemplative prayer is not on the level of thinking. It is consenting with your will to God's Presence in pure faith.

Emotionally charged thoughts are the chief way that the unconscious has of expelling chunks of emotional junk. In this way, without your perceiving it, a great many emotional conflicts that are hidden in your unconscious and affecting your decisions more than you realize are being resolved. As a consequence, over a period of time you will feel a greater sense of well-being and inner freedom. The very thoughts that you lament while in prayer are freeing the psyche from the damage that has accumulated in your nervous system over a lifetime. In this prayer both thoughts and silence have an important role to play.

To use a clumsy simile, in tenement houses where the garbage collection is unreliable, some tenants use the bathroom to store the garbage. If you want to take a bath, the first thing you have to do is empty out the junk. A similar procedure holds in this prayer. When we commit ourselves to the spiritual journey, the first thing the Spirit does is start removing the emotional junk inside of us. He wishes to fill us completely and to transform our entire body-spirit organism into a flexible instrument of divine love. But as long as we have obstacles in us, some of which we are not even aware, he can't fill us to capacity. In his love and zeal he begins to clean out the tub. One means by which he does this is by means of the passive purification initiated by the dynamic of contemplative prayer.

Centering prayer, insofar as it puts us at God's disposal, is a kind of request that He take our purification in hand. It takes courage to face up to the process of self-knowledge, but it is the only way of getting in touch with our true identity and ultimately with our true Self. When you feel bored, restless, and that anything would be better than just sitting still and being battered by thoughts, stay there anyhow. It's like being out in the rain without an umbrella and getting drenched to the skin. There is no use groaning because you didn't bring your umbrella. The best approach is simply to be willing to be doused by the torrent of your thoughts. Say, "I am going to get wet," and enjoy the rain. Before you reflect on whether a particular period of prayer is going well, you are having a good period of prayer. After you reflect, it is not so good. If you are drenched with thoughts and can't do anything about it, acquiesce to the fact that that's the way it is for today. The less you wiggle and scream, the sooner the work can be done. Tomorrow or a few days from now will be better. The capacity to accept what comes down the stream of consciousness is an essential part of the discipline. Cultivate a neutral attitude toward the psychological content of your prayer. Then it won't bother you whether you have thoughts. Offer your powerlessness to God and wait peacefully in His Presence. All thoughts pass if you wait long enough.

Another point that is worth remembering. During the unloading process sometimes you may want to figure out where a particular smile, itch, pain, or strong feeling is coming from in your psyche and to identify it with some earlier period in your life. That's useless. The nature of the unloading process is that it does not focus on any particular event. It loosens up all the rubbish, so to speak, and the psychological refuse comes up as a kind of compost. It's like throwing out the garbage. You don't separate the egg shells from the orange peels. You just throw the whole thing out. Nobody is asking you to look through it or try to evaluate it. You just throw everything out together in one big garbage bag.

It can also happen that external difficulties may arise in your life that have a direct connection with your spiritual growth. They are another way God uses to bring you to a deeper knowledge of yourself and to a greater compassion for your family, friends, and other people.

> I think I've been using the prayer words as a way of resisting thoughts. I'm not sure what it means to sink into a disturbing emotion without holding on to it.

One way to deal with intense restlessness, physical pain, or emotions, such as fear or anxiety, that arise at such times of unloading is to rest in the painful feeling for a minute or two and allow the pain itself to be your prayer word. In other words, one of the best ways of letting go of an emotion is simply to feel it. Painful emotions, even some physical pains, tend to disintegrate when fully accepted. Other manifestations of the unstressing experience may be an itch, tears, or laughter. Some people have been known to have a fit of laughter in the middle of centering prayer. Perhaps there was a joke they heard long ago that they were unable to enjoy because of some defense mechanism, and they finally were humble enough or free enough to get the point. You may also find yourself dissolved in tears for no reason at all. An old grief that wasn't allowed expression at the proper time is at last being felt. Contemplative prayer has a way of completing everything unfinished in your life by allowing the emotions to have an outlet in the form of moods or thoughts that seem but a jumble. This is the dynamic of purification. The intensity of feelings of fear, anxiety, or anger may have no relationship to your recent experience. Sitting through that kind of stuff is more useful than consoling experiences. The purpose of centering prayer is not to experience peace but to evacuate the unconscious obstacles to the permanent abiding state of union with God. Not contemplative *prayer* but the contemplative *state* is the purpose of our practice; not experiences, however exotic or reassuring, but the permanent and abiding awareness of God that comes through the mysterious restructuring of consciousness. At some point in your life, it could be in the middle of the night, on a subway, or in the midst of prayer, the necessary changes in the nervous system and psyche finally come to completion. That particular stage of the spiritual journey resolves itself, and you no longer have the problems that you had before. The restructuring of consciousness is the fruit of regular practice. That is why it makes no sense to aim at particular experiences. You can't even imagine a state of consciousness that you've never had before, so it is a waste of time and energy to anticipate it. The practice will eventually bring about the change of consciousness. The most significant happening at this stage of the journey is the calming of the affective system. You become free of emotional swings because the false self system on which they were based has at last been dismantled. The emotions then come through in their purity and are no longer upsetting. This is a marvelous release from inner turmoil.

When you feel restless, agitated, or pained by some emotional experience, you can't spend the time better than by waiting it out. The temptation is great when you are suffering from a distressing emotion to try to push it away. However, by allowing your attention to move gently toward the emotion and by sinking into it, as though you were getting into a nice jacuzzi, you are embracing God in the feeling. Don't think; just feel the emotion.

If you were blind and then got your sight back, even the ugliest things would be appreciated. Suppose you had no emotions and suddenly experienced one; even a disagreeable emotion would be thrilling. Actually, no emotion is really distressing; it is only the false self that interprets it as distressing. Emotional swings are gradually dissolved by the complete acceptance of them. To put this into practice, you must first recognize and identify the emotion: "Yes, I am angry, I am panicky, terrified, restless." Every feeling has some good. Since God is the ground of everything, we know that even the feeling of guilt, in a certain sense, is God. If you can embrace the painful feeling, whatever it is, as if it were God, you are uniting yourself with God, because anything that has reality has God as its foundation. "Letting go" is not a simple term; it is quite subtle and has important nuances—depending on what you are intending to let go of. When a thought is not disturbing, letting go means paying no attention to it. When a thought is disturbing, it won't go away so easily, so you have to let it go in some other way. One way you can let it go is to sink into it and identify with it, out of love for God. This may not be possible at first, but try it and see what happens. The principal discipline of contemplative prayer is letting go.

To sum up what I have said on this fifth kind of thought, contemplative prayer is part of a reality that is bigger than itself. It is part of the whole process of integration, which requires opening to God at the level of the unconscious. This releases a dynamic that will be peaceful at times, and at other times heavily laden with thoughts and emotion. Both experiences are part of the same process of integration and healing. Each kind of experience, therefore, should be accepted with the same peace, gratitude, and confidence in God. Both are necessary to complete the process of transformation.

If you are suffering from a barrage of thoughts from the unconscious, you don't have to articulate the sacred word clearly in your imagination or keep repeating it in a frantic effort to stabilize your mind. You should think it as easily as you think any thought that comes to mind spontaneously.

Do not resist any thought, do not hang on to any thought, do not react emotionally to any thought. This is the proper response to all five kinds of thoughts that come down the stream of consciousness.

> When I came out of prayer, I found I had been crying, but I wasn't sad. I didn't perceive myself as being sad during any part of the meditation.

You might be consoled to know that Benedict of Nursia, the founder of Western monasticism, wept almost continuously. This was his characteristic response to the goodness of God. Similarly, there are times when we can't say anything, think anything, or feel anything. The only response is to dissolve in the presence of God's incredible goodness.

Tears may express joy as well as sorrow. They may also indicate the release of a whole bundle of emotions that can't find expression in any other way. In prayer if tears come, treat them as a gift, a response to God's goodness, which is both painful and joyful at the same time. Joy can be so great that it is painful.

It is good not to make too much of any experience or insight during prayer itself. Afterward you can reflect on it, but during prayer if you notice tears falling, lips smiling, eyes twitching, itches, and pains—treat them like any other thought and let them all go by. Gently return to the sacred word. This prayer is an apprenticeship in letting go of our dependency on thinking in order to know God in interior silence. The obstacles to getting there have to be unloaded in one way or another. Thoughts, moods, or feelings of depression that might last for several days are ways the psyche has of evacuating the undigested emotional material of a lifetime. When these pass, your psychological insides will feel much better. It's like being nauseated; it is disagreeable while your dinner is coming up, but afterwards you feel great.

Of course, if a physical pain lasts throughout the whole period of prayer, you may actually have some pathology and need to see a doctor. But often it is just an emotional knot rooted in your physiology that is unwinding, and it takes the form of a brief pain, tears, or laughter. I know people who were overcome by laughter in their prayer. I guess they hit something in the unconscious they never thought was funny before and finally got the joke. Through the deepening of one's trust in God, one is able to acknowledge the dark places in one's personality according to one's own natural rhythm. A good therapist will not bring up painful insights until he or she sees that the patient is ready to face them. God is the same way. As humility and trust deepen, you can acknowledge the dark side of your personality more easily. Eventually you will reach the center of your human poverty and powerlessness and feel happy to be there. Then you enter into the freedom of God's creative action because there is no longer any selfish or possessive attitude toward your personality or talents. You are completely at God's disposal. Interior freedom is the goal of this prayer. Not freedom to do what you like, but freedom to do what God likes—freedom to be your true Self and to be transformed in Christ.

There seems to be a dimension in the prayer of quiet that is healing. At least that is my experience. Some people do not have too
much to heal. But if there are big scars, the prayer of quiet seems
to be a very soothing ointment for these wounds.

Yes, that is one important effect. John of the Cross taught that interior
silence is the place where the Spirit secretly anoints the soul and heals
our deepest wounds.

Does the healing extend to the body as well as the soul?

Illnesses that are largely psychosomatic can certainly be healed by bringing peace to one's emotional life.

I was thinking that God has a way of concealing His work in us from
our own eyes, leaving us with something like St. Paul's thorn of the
flesh, to keep us humble.

Contemplative prayer doesn't establish people in glory, that's for sure,
but it helps them to bear infirmities such as you mentioned. If certain types
of people have too much success in their prayer, they may need a little tug
to bring them down to earth once in a while.

The method of centering prayer is only an entrance into contemplative
prayer. As one's experience of the latter develops, it becomes more difficult
to speak about because it doesn't enter into the ordinary experience of the
psychic life as such. Imagine the rays of the sun in a pool of water. The
sun's rays are united to the water, yet at the same time they are quite distinct
from it. They are coming from a different place. Similarly, one's experience
of God in contemplative prayer is not easy to make distinctions about. The
less you can say about it, the more likely it is present. It is in all and through
all. And so it kind of falls out of sight.

The beginning of anything is always striking, but as you get used to
it or when it becomes a part of you, you begin to take it for granted. It
no longer stirs up the emotional dust that it did when it was a new experience. The same thing happens at the beginning of the spiritual journey.

For some people, contemplative prayer can be very mysterious indeed. They themselves can't say anything about what they experience except that it is real for them. The kind of infirmities that you mention, which are obvious both to them and to others, are a wonderful means of hiding them from themselves as well as from others. God loves to hide the holiness of His friends, especially from themselves.

> As people grow in the prayer life, do they still experience an alternation of thoughts and contemplative moments?

As the unconscious empties out, the fruits of an integrated human nature and the resulting free flow of grace will manifest themselves by a significant change of attitude. The union that one discovers in contemplative prayer will not be reserved to that time. Moments of silence will overtake you in the course of daily life. Reality will tend to become more transparent. Its divine Source will shine through it.

When everything in the unconscious is emptied out, the kinds of thoughts that were passing by in the beginning will no longer exist. There is an end to the process of purification. Then the awareness of union with God will be continuous because there will be no obstacle in our conscious or unconscious life to interfere with it. There is nothing wrong with reality. The problem is with us, who cannot relate to it properly because of the obstacles in us. When all the obstacles are emptied out, the light of God's presence will illumine our spirit all the time, even when we are immersed in activity. Instead of being overwhelmed by externals, the true Self, now in union with God, will dominate them.

Perhaps the first stage in the development of contemplative prayer is the awareness of our independence from our ordinary psychological world. In other words, we are aware that we are not just our body and that we are not just our thoughts and feelings. We are no longer so identified with external objects that we can think of nothing else. We are becoming aware of our spiritual nature. Our spirit is the dwelling place of the Trinity. That realization remains part of every other reality and is no longer overwhelmed, even in the midst of great activity, by circumstances, external objects or our emotions and thoughts.

But the experience of independence and distancing from the rest of reality is not an absolute independence. It is only the affirmation of our true Self. Another awareness follows as a further development. As the unconscious is emptied out, the awareness of the deepest level in us is also an awareness of the deepest level in everyone else. This is the basis for the commandment to love one's neighbor as oneself. When you truly love yourself, you become aware that your true Self is Christ expressing himself in you, and the further awareness that everybody else enjoys this potential too. Augustine had a phrase for it: "One Christ loving himself." That is a good description of a mature Christian community. You are aware that a power greater than you is doing everything.

Then everything begins to reflect not only its own beauty but also the beauty of its Source. One becomes united to everything else in which God dwells. The insight into Christ dwelling in every other person enables one to express charity toward others with greater spontaneity. Instead of seeing only someone's personality, race, nationality, gender, status, or characteristics (which you like or do not like), you see what is deepest—one's union or potential union with Christ. You also perceive everyone's desperate need of help. The transcendent potential of most people is still waiting to be realized, and this awakens a great sense of compassion. This Christ-centered love takes us out of ourselves and brings our newly found sense of independence into relationships that are not based on dependency, as many relationships tend to be, but that are based on Christ as their center. It enables one to work for others with great liberty of spirit because one is no longer seeking one's own ego-centered goals but responding to reality as it is.

Divine love is not an attitude that one puts on like a cloak. It is rather the right way to respond to reality. It is the right relationship to being, including our own being. And that relationship is primarily one of receiving. No one has any degree of divine love except what one has received. An important part of the response to divine love, once it has been received, is to pass it on to our neighbor in a way that is appropriate in the present moment.

> Is the purpose of this prayer to keep you in a state of union with God throughout the day?

Yes, but in the beginning it is not likely to be continuous. Later on, as prayer develops, a closer union in daily life becomes more evident. One can also be in union with God without any form of recollection that affects the senses. This is what I mean by preparing the body for higher states of consciousness. Physical ecstasy is a weakness of the body. When the senses are not ready to endure the intensity of God's communications, they just give way and one is rapt out of the body. Mature mystics who have passed through that stage rarely have bodily ecstasies. They have integrated spiritual communications with their physical nature and the body is now strong enough to receive them without the former inconveniences. Living the divine life becomes like living ordinary human life. If you are familiar with the *Ten Ox Pictures* of Zen, the last one represents the return to ordinary life after full enlightenment. It symbolizes the fact that there is no way to distinguish the life with which you started from what it has become, except that it is totally transformed in its ordinariness.

The triumph of grace enables people to live their ordinary lives divinely. First come moments of recollection that are absorbing. After these have been thoroughly integrated, the same graces are given without one's being absorbed by them. One is completely free for one's ordinary daily activities with the same degree (or greater) of union with God that one had before. Continuous prayer in the fullest sense of the term is present when the motivation of all our actions is coming from the Spirit. Short of that state, we have to use methods to unite us to God.

There is a difference between *being* and *doing*. Once one's being is transformed into Christ, all one's doing becomes anointed with the interior transformation of one's being. I suppose this is the mystery of Mother Teresa's great charm. She fascinates people. Cameras follow her not because she is physically beautiful, but because she is radiating the mysterious attractiveness of God. I'm sure she is not trying to do so, but because she is so, it happens. This is the kind of transformation contemplative prayer tends to produce. It is easy to bog down at lower levels of spiritual development. The challenge always comes to go farther, and if we accept, we are off to the races again.

No one ever grew as much in the spiritual life as the Blessed Virgin Mary because there was no interior obstacle to hinder her growth. Growing in grace for her meant growing in the midst of the human condition with its interminable trials. She had, in fact, the heaviest kinds of trials. The transforming union should enable one to handle greater trials than those of less evolved Christians. What's the use of building this magnificent spiritual building unless you do something with it? I am sure God doesn't intend merely to look at these people who are so holy. He wants them to do something. If He liberated them from their false selves, it was precisely for some great purpose.

Suppose one has reached inner resurrection, transforming union, and no longer experiences the turmoil of one's emotions because they have all been transmuted into virtues. Christ is living in such persons in a remarkable way, and they are aware of their permanent union with him. Suppose God should then ask them to give up that state of enlightenment and to go back to the kind of trials, or worse, they they endured before. Their union with God would remain, but it would be completely hidden from them on the psychic level. This is one form of vicarious suffering. The transforming union is not a free ticket to happiness in this world. For some, this may mean a life of complete solitude full of loneliness; for others, it may mean an active apostolate that prevents them from enjoying the delights of divine union; for others again, it may mean intense suffering—physical, mental or spiritual—which they undergo for some special intention or for the whole human family. Their transformed humanity makes their sufferings of immense value for the same reason that Jesus, because of his divine dignity, became the Savior of every human being, past, present, and future.

Therese of Lisieux during her last illness could no longer think of heaven, although up until then it had been her greatest joy. Yet she had clearly reached transforming union, attested to by the piercing of her heart. As she herself was dimly aware, she was passing through another dark night for the unbelievers of her time. She lived at the crest of the rationalistic age when the arrogance of the human intellect was probably at its height.

Thus the greatest trials of the spiritual journey may occur *after* the transforming union. They would not take away the union, but the union would be so pure that, like a ray of light passing through a perfect vacuum, it would not be perceived. This would be a most profound way of imitating the Son of God, who gave up being God, as Paul said, in order to take upon himself the consequences of the human condition. Jesus relinquished the privileges of his unique union with the Father in order to experience our weakness and to make our sufferings his own. That sacrifice could only be imitated by one who has achieved divine union and who then, at God's request or insistence, gives back to God all the normal enjoyment of that state to be immersed once again in unbearable trials. This is evident in the lives of a number of mystics and saints. And I dare say God isn't going to change His way of doing things.

Life, once one is in union with God, is what God wants it to be. It is full of surprises. You can be sure that whatever you expect to happen will not happen. That is the only thing of which you can be certain in the spiritual journey. It is by giving up all your expectations that you will be led to Medicine Lake, the Native American's term for contemplative prayer. The medicine that everyone needs is contemplation, which alone leads to transformation.

Contemplative prayer will go through various stages and vicissitudes. You may have experiences that will leave you in confusion. The Lord will bring help to you through a book, a person, or your own patience. Sometimes it is God's will to leave you alone without any help. You may have to learn to live with impossible situations. People who can live peacefully in impossible situations will make great headway in the spiritual journey. You will come up against loneliness and existential dread. You may feel as if nobody in the world understands you or could help you and that God is a billion light-years away. All these things are part of the preparation process. God is like a farmer preparing the soil of our soul to bear not just forty-fold or sixtyfold, but a hundredfold. That means that the soil has to be well tilled. It is as if God drives His tractor over the field of our soul and harrows it in one direction, then in the opposite direction, and then He goes around in a circle. He keeps doing the same thing again and again until the soil becomes as fine as sand. When all is ready, the seed is sown.

Or take the image of a growing tree. At first you see the trunk and the branches. Later come the leaves. This makes the tree beautiful, the stage of growth that might be compared to the enjoyment that comes when you first learn how to enter into interior silence. After the leaves come the flowers, another moment of intense satisfaction. But they quickly die and fall to the ground. The fruit comes only at the end of the season, and even then it takes a while for it to ripen on the tree. So don't think when the leaves appear and the flowers come, that this is the end of the journey. The spiritual journey is a long trip.

Moreover, your experience will seem to recycle and you'll feel that you are back to where you started and haven't made any progress at all. Recycling is like climbing a spiral staircase. You seem to be returning to the point from which you started, but in actual fact you are at a higher level. An eagle rising toward the sun keeps returning to the same place on the horizontal plane, but to a higher place on the vertical plane.

The inflowing of the divine light into our souls is a ray of darkness according to John of the Cross. We see light in a dark room is because of the dust that is there. If there were no dust, the ray of light would go right through the room without being observed. This is a symbol of the full development of contemplative prayer, which is so pure that it is not perceptible to the one receiving it. It is manifest, however, in the progressive transformation of the person. Such a person manifests God more than any sacrament.

Is this not the meaning of the Feast of the Immaculate Conception? We are invited to become what Our Lady was from the beginning, a pure transmission of God's presence and action. Contemplative prayer is the school through which we pass to come to the contemplative state, the means God normally uses to bring people to an abiding state of union. Once in that state they may not have much awareness of God's inflowing graces, but the Holy Spirit is the inspiration or motivation of all they do.

CHAPTER TEN

Summary of the Centering Prayer Method

The method of centering prayer is a way of reducing the ordinary obstacles to contemplation and preparing the human faculties to cooperate with this gift. It is an attempt to present the teaching of earlier times in an up-dated format and to put a certain order and regularity into it. It is not meant to replace all other kinds of prayer. But it puts the other kinds of prayer into a new perspective. During the time of prayer it centers one's attention on God's presence within. At other times one's attention moves outward to discover His presence everywhere else. Centering prayer is not an end in itself, but a beginning. It is not done for the sake of having an experience, but for the sake of its positive fruits in one's life.

The method of centering prayer is designed to turn off the ordinary flow of thoughts, that reinforces our habitual way of thinking of ourselves and of looking at the world. It is like turning a radio from long wave to short wave. You may be used to a long wave set and the stations it picks up but if you want to hear stations from far away, you have to turn to the other wavelength. In similar fashion, if you turn off your ordinary thinking and emotional patterns, you open yourself to a new world of reality.

THE METHOD

To do this systematically, take up a comfortable position that will enable you to sit still. Close your eyes. Half of the world disappears for we generally think most about what we see. In order to slow down the usual flow of thoughts, think just one thought. For this purpose choose a word of one or two syllables with which you feel comfortable.

A general loving look toward God may be better suited to the disposition of some persons. But the same procedures are followed as in the use of the sacred word. The word is a sacred word because it is the symbol of your intention to open yourself to the mystery of God's presence beyond thoughts, images and emotions. It is chosen not for its content but for its intent. It is merely a pointer that expresses the direction of your inward movement toward the presence of God.

To start, introduce the sacred word in your imagination as gently as if you were laying a feather on a piece of absorbent cotton. Keep thinking the sacred word in whatever form it arises. It is not meant to be repeated continuously. The word can flatten out, become vague or just an impulse of the will, or even disappear. Accept it in whatever form it arises.

When you become aware that you are thinking some other thought, return to the sacred word as the expression of your intent. The effectiveness of this prayer does not depend on how distinctly you say the sacred word or how often, but rather on the gentleness with which you introduce it into your imagination in the beginning and the promptness with which you return to it when you are hooked on some other thought.

Thoughts are an inevitable part of centering prayer. Our ordinary thoughts are like boats sitting on a river so closely packed together that we cannot see the river that is holding them up. A "thought" in the context of this prayer is any perception that crosses the inner screen of consciousness. We are normally aware of one object after another passing across the inner screen of consciousness: images, memories, feelings, external impressions. When we slow down that flow for a little while, space begins to appear between the boats. Up comes the reality on which they are floating.

The prayer of centering is a method of directing your attention from the particular to the general, from the concrete to the formless. At first you are preoccupied by the boats that are going by. You become interested in seeing what is on them. But just let them all go by. If you catch yourself becoming interested in them, return to the sacred word as the expression of the movement of your whole being toward God present within you.

The sacred word is a simple thought that you are thinking at ever deepening levels of perception. That's why you accept the sacred word in whatever form it arises within you. The word on your lips is exterior and has no part in this form of prayer. The thought in your imagination is interior; the word as an impulse of your will is more interior still. Only when you pass beyond the word into pure awareness is the process of interiorization complete. That is what Mary of Bethany was doing at the feet of Jesus. She was going beyond the words she was hearing to the Person who was speaking and entering into union with Him. This is what we are doing as we sit in centering prayer interiorizing the sacred word. We are going beyond the sacred word into union with that to which it points—the Ultimate Mystery, the Presence of God, beyond any perception that we can form of Him.

FIVE TYPES OF THOUGHTS

Various kinds of thoughts may come down the stream of consciousness when we start to quiet our mind. The appropriate response to each one varies according to the thought.

1. *The woolgathering of the imagination.* The most obvious thoughts are the superficial ones that the imagination grinds out because of its natural propensity for perpetual motion. It is important just to accept them and not to pay any undue attention to them. Such thoughts are like the noise in the street floating through the window of an apartment where two people are carrying on a conversation. Their attention is firmly directed to each other, but they cannot avoid hearing the street noise. Sometimes they reach a point where they don't notice it at all. At other times the honking of horns may distract them momentarily. The only reasonable attitude is to put up with the noise and pay as little attention to it as possible. In this way they give as much of their undivided attention to each other as circumstances allow.

2. *Thoughts with an emotional attraction to them.* The second kind of thought occurs when you get interested in something that is happening in the street. A brawl breaks out and attracts your curiosity. This is the kind of thought that calls for some reaction. Returning gently to the sacred

word is a means of getting back to the general loving attention you were offering to God. It is important not to be annoyed with yourself if you get involved with these interesting thoughts. Any annoyance that you give in to is another thought, and will take you farther away from the interior silence that is the proximate goal of this prayer.

3. *Insights, and psychological breakthroughs.* A third kind of thought arises as we sink into deep peace and interior silence. Something in our minds goes fishing. What seem to be brilliant theological insights and marvelous psychological breakthroughs, like tasty bait, are dangled in front of our mind's eye and we think, "I must take a moment to make sure I grasp this fantastic insight!" If you acquiesce to a thought of this nature long enough to fix it in your memory you will be drawn out of the deep, refreshing waters of interior silence. Any deliberate thought brings you out.

A very intimate kind of self-denial is necessary in this prayer. It is not just an experience of refreshment—a sort of spiritual happy hour—though this can be a side-effect. It involves the denial of what we are most attached to, namely, our own inmost thoughts and feelings and the source from which they come, the false self.

This kind of asceticism goes to the roots of our attachment to the emotional programming of the false self. It is a thorough and delightful kind of self-denial, which does not have to be afflictive to be effective. The question is how to choose the most useful and appropriate kind of self-denial and how to work at it.

4. *Self-reflection.* As you settle into deep peace and freedom from particular thoughts, a desire to reflect on what is happening may arise. You may think, "At last I am getting some place!" or, "This feeling is just great!" or, "If only I could make a mental note of how I got here so that I can get back to it whenever I want!" These are examples of the fourth kind of thought. You are being offered a choice between reflecting on what is going on and letting go of the experience. If you let go, you go into deeper interior silence. If you reflect, you come out and have to start over. There will be a lot of starting over.

Reflection is one step back from experience. It is a photograph of reality. As soon as you start to reflect on an experience, it is over. Reflection on joy is an attempt to possess it. Then it is lost. The tendency to reflect is one of the hardest things to handle in contemplative prayer. We want to savor the moment of pure joy, pure experience, pure awareness. We want to reflect on moments of deep peace or union in order to remember how we got there and thus how to get back. But if you can let this temptation go by and return to the sacred word, you will pass to a new level of freedom, a more refined joy.

The presence of God is like the air we breathe. You can have all you want of it as long as you do not try to take possession of it and hang on to it.

This prayer is communion with the Spirit of God, who is Charity, pure gift. Our possessive instinct wants to hang on for dear life to what is pleasant—and nothing is more delightful than the divine Presence; it brings such a deep sense of security and tranquillity. The Presence of God does not respond to greed. It is totally available, but on condition that we accept it freely and do not try to possess it.

This method of prayer is a learning of self-surrender. It teaches us through our many mistakes not to be possessive but to let go. If, in this prayer, you can get over the inveterate habit of reflecting on what is going on, if you can have peace and not think about having it, then you will have learned how to do it.

5. *Interior Purification.* Any form of meditation or prayer that transcends thinking sets off the dynamic of interior purification. This dynamic is God's school of psychotherapy. It enables the organism to release deep rooted tension in the form of thoughts. Generally, thoughts that result from this therapy arise without one's knowing where they come from or why. They introduce themselves with a certain force or emotional charge. One may feel intense anger, sorrow or fear without any relation to the recent past. Once again, the best way to handle them is to return to the sacred word.

Through this process, the undigested psychological material of a lifetime is gradually evacuated, the emotional investment of early childhood in programs for happiness based on instinctual drives is dismantled, and the false self gives way to the true self.

Once you grasp the fact that thoughts are not only inevitable, but an integral part of the process of healing and growth initiated by God, you are able to take a positive view of them. Instead of looking upon them as painful distractions, you see them in a broader perspective that includes both interior silence and thoughts—thoughts that you do not want, but which, are just as valuable for the purpose of purification, as moments of profound tranquility.

RESTING IN GOD

As you quiet down and go deeper, you may reach a place where the sacred word disappears altogether and there are no thoughts. This is often experienced as a suspension of consciousness, a space. The next thing you are aware of is the thought, "Where was I? There was no sacred word and I wasn't thinking." Or you may experience it as a place outside of time. Time is the measure of motion. If the ordinary flow of thoughts is reduced to where there are few or no successive thoughts, the time of prayer passes like a snap of the fingers.

The experience of interior silence or "resting in God" is beyond thinking, images, and emotions. This awareness tells you that the core of your being is eternal and indestructible and that you as a person are loved by God and share his divine life. Many people habitually enjoy the clear experience of interior silence during prayer. Others habitually experience calm and tranquillity along with a trickle of thoughts at the same time. Still others rarely have such experiences. In whatever form or degree interior silence occurs, it is to be accepted but not desired, for the feeling of desire would be a thought.

CONCLUSION

Take everything that happens during the periods of centering prayer peacefully and gratefully, without putting a judgement on anything. Even if you should have an overwhelming experience of God, this is not the time to think about it. Let the thoughts come and go. The basic principle for handling thoughts in this prayer is this: Resist no thought, hang on to no thought, react emotionally to no thought. Whatever image, feeling, reflection, or experience attracts your attention, return to the sacred word.

Don't judge centering prayer on the basis of how many thoughts come or how much peace you enjoy. The only way to judge this prayer is by its long-range fruits: whether in daily life you enjoy greater peace, humility and charity. Having come to deep interior silence, you begin to relate to others beyond the superficial aspects of social status, race, nationality, religion, and personal characteristics.

To know God in this way is to perceive a new dimension to all reality. The ripe fruit of contemplative prayer is to bring back into the humdrum routines of daily life not just the thought of God, but the spontaneous awareness of His abiding Presence in, through, and beyond everything. *HE WHO IS*—the infinite, incomprehensible, and ineffable One—is the God of pure faith. In this prayer we confront the most fundamental human question: "Who are you, Lord?"—and wait for the answer.

CHAPTER ELEVEN

The Intensive Centering Prayer Experience

In a retreat setting, the length of the periods of centering prayer can be extended. Members of a group that regularly practices centering prayer together may also wish to increase the time length of the prayer periods once a week or once a month.

Following is a report of participants that reflects the usual experiences of persons after three successive periods of centering.

Lengthening or multiplying periods of centering prayer can help to deepen the experience of interior silence. In such a context it may accelerate the process of unloading the unconscious. The following is a report of one of these sessions in which there were three twenty-minute periods of centering separated by a five to seven minute meditative walk in single file at a very slow and deliberate pace.

RETREATANT 1: I found it to be a very peaceful experience. The continuity of three sustained periods brought about a deeper feeling of peace. There was no break at all, even though we got up and walked around. I can't over-emphasize the experience of a community type of prayer. I got a deeper insight into sharing prayer, any type of prayer.

RESPONSE: Actually, the walking is meant to be part of the prayer, a first step to bringing interior silence into activity of a very simple kind.

RETREATANT 2: I found it very, very peaceful, but I was also aware of how many thoughts I was getting in the three periods. They did not disturb the peace, but I was aware of how many there were. I also had a sensation that sometimes my whole body wanted to go deeper. I found the time went very fast.

RETREATANT 3: The first insight that I had today was the fact that there was a supportive element in group prayer. I have practiced centering prayer for about two years alone, and I could not fathom how it could be done in a group, so I had my doubts. But they have been dissolved.

RETREATANT 4: During the first period of prayer I felt restless, more than I had before, but when I got to the third one, it was peaceful. It was an answer to a question that I have had for a long time. I have often found that my time span for prayer is on the short side, maybe twenty to twenty-five minutes. I have wondered whether it should lengthen with time. It has not and I was worried. But I can see from this experience that with this little break in between, it can be prolonged.

RETREATANT 5: I must say that the time went by very quickly and the walk tended to recharge my batteries. When I came back for the second period, the time went by even more quickly, and so for the third.

RESPONSE: The deeper the silence you have, the faster the time goes. After all, what is time? It is just the measurement of objects of perception going by. So when there are fewer objects, there is less time. At least there is less awareness of time. When nothing is going by, there is no sense of time at all, and that is when prayer is over like a flash. Such deep prayer is an intuition into what eternity is like. It is a preview of death, not death in a morbid sense, but in a delightful sense.

RETREATANT 6: In the beginning, I was deliberately trying to be quiet, and I was getting in my own way. Somehow or other, in the second or third period, I was experiencing great ease and a conscious sensation of quiet joy.

RETREATANT 7: At the beginning, it was rather tedious, but part way through the afternoon, I felt a subtle breakthrough, or just an ease of being without any interior pressure.

RESPONSE: If you keep centering long enough, your resistance gets tired and you fall into what you are supposed to be doing anyway. Thus, there is an advantage in gently tiring yourself out.

RETREATANT 8: I found the third meditation too short.

RESPONSE: Depending on one's temperament or grace, the time span can be lengthened when one is alone. But for a group of people, it is better to agree on a certain amount of time that is not too short and not too long. It must be long enough to enable your faculties to get into it and quiet down. But not so long that it discourages the faint-hearted, who will never do it if they have to face something that looks endless to them. Three successive periods with a brief, contemplative walk in between is a way of initiating ourselves into the fact that we are perfectly capable of an extended period of resting in God.

RETREATANT 9: I found a deep rest; so much so, that I was not sure if I was sleeping, at least part of the time. In the beginning, I was not sure if I could do the three of them in a row. It was not all that difficult once I got into it. I am still not sure what to do with the sacred word, whether there should be an effort on my part to repeat it, or just to let it go.

RESPONSE: The main thing to keep in mind in this prayer is that there is no effort, there is only the very gentle activity of listening. It is almost like letting the word say itself. But letting go of that activity is even better. Whenever you are uncertain what to do, you are completely free to do either, and your own experience will teach you. Just keep in mind that silence is better than the sacred word. Or to put it another way, it *is* the sacred word at the deepest level. Whenever you come back to the sacred word, it should be as easily as possible, as if it were a spontaneous thought that just came along. It does not have to be explicit or articulated. Even the thought to return to the sacred word may be enough.

RETREATANT 10: I found myself using the word less today than I have ever used it before.

RESPONSE: Its use or presence will vary from one period of prayer to the next, according to circumstances. You need great flexibility in using it. The principle is always to use it to go toward greater peace, silence, and beyond. But when one is in peace, silence, and beyond, forget it.

RETREATANT 11: I found myself going deeper and deeper in each session, and I have a question. Every morning I do my centering prayer, and then I offer Mass. But I find it hard to come out of it. What should I do?

RESPONSE: That's a nice problem to have.

RETREATANT 11: But should I not be thinking of the prayers of the Mass? Instead I find myself centering.

RESPONSE: If the divine Presence overtakes you and you are not leading the assembly, there is no reason why you cannot rest in the Presence of God. If you have some function to fulfill—if you are the principal celebrant, for example—obviously you have to move things along. You cannot just let the congregation wait until you come out of it.

RETREATANT 11: The problem is that I am enjoying this more than anything else.

RESPONSE: There are times in one's life when the divine action is very strong and hard to resist. There are also times when the Lord seems to forget about you. The main things is to accept whatever comes, to adjust to what happens, to whatever He gives you. By alternating the sense of His closeness and distance, God trains our faculties to accept the mystery of His Presence beyond any kind of sensible or conceptual experience. The divine Presence is very close and immediate, when we are doing the most ordinary actions. Faith should become so transparent that it does not need experience. But it takes a lot of experience to reach that point.

As God brings the "new man" to life in interior silence, that is to say, the new you, with the world view that Christ shares with you in deep silence, His view of things becomes more important to you than your own. Then He asks you to live that new life in the circumstances of everyday life, in your daily routine, contradicted by noise, opposition, and anxieties. These seem to persecute you because you want to be alone to relish that silence. But it is important to allow oneself to be confronted by daily life. The alternation between deep silence and action gradually brings the two together. You become fully integrated, a contemplative and yet fully capable of action at the same time. You are Mary and Martha at once.

We all have these two capacities, but they are in different proportions. By bringing each of them to its full potential and integrating them, one becomes a mature Christian, able to bring forth out of one's tool kit old things and new. It is to be able to act and to be able not to act, to come into function and to withdraw into silence. The alternation of contemplative prayer and action gradually establishes you in the contemplative dimension of the Gospel, which is a new and transformed state of consciousness.

CHAPTER TWELVE

Methods of Extending the Effects of Contemplative Prayer Into Daily Life

Centering prayer is the keystone of a comprehensive commitment to the contemplative dimensions of the Gospel. Two periods a day of twenty to thirty minutes—one in the early morning and one halfway through the day or in the early evening—maintain the reservoir of interior silence at a high level at all times. Those who have more time at their disposal might begin with a brief reading of ten or fifteen minutes from the Gospel. For those who wish to give a full hour in the morning to interior silence, start with ten minutes of Gospel reading and then center for twenty minutes. Do a slow, meditative walk around the room for five to seven minutes; sit down and do a second period of centering. You still have ten minutes for planning your day, praying for others, or conversing with the Lord.

To find time for a second period later in the day may require special effort. If you have to be available to your family as soon as you walk in the door, you might center during your lunch hour. Or you might stop on the way home from work and center in a church or park. If it is impossible to get a second period of prayer in, it is important that you lengthen the first one. There are a number of practices that can help maintain your reservoir of interior silence throughout the day and thus extend its effects into ordinary activities.

MEANS OF EXTENDING THE EFFECTS
OF CENTERING PRAYER INTO DAILY LIFE

1. *Cultivate a basic acceptance of yourself.* Have a genuine compassion for yourself, including all your past history, failings, limitations, and sins. Expect to make many mistakes. But learn from them. To learn from experience is the path to wisdom.

2. *Pick a prayer for action.* This is a five to nine-syllable sentence from scripture that you gradually work into your subconscious by repeating it mentally at times when your mind is relatively free, such as while washing up, doing light chores, walking, driving, waiting, etc. Synchronize it with your heartbeat. Eventually it says itself and thus maintains a link with your reservoir of interior silence throughout the day. If you have a tendency to scrupulosity and feel a compulsion to say the prayer over and over or if frequent repetition brings on a headache or a backache, this practice is not for you.[1]

3. *Spend time daily listening to the Word of God in lectio divina.* Give fifteen minutes or longer every day to the reading of the New Testament or a spiritual book that speaks to your heart.

4. *Carry a "Minute Book".* This is a series of short readings—a sentence or two, or at most a paragraph—from your favorite spiritual writers or from your own journal that reminds you of your commitment to Christ and to contemplative prayer. Carry it in your pocket or purse and when you have a stray minute or two, read a few lines.

5. *Deliberately dismantle the emotional programming of the false self.* Observe the emotions that most upset you and the events that set them off, but without analyzing, rationalizing, or justifying your reactions. Name the chief emotion you are feeling and the particular event that triggered it and release the energy that is building up by a strong act of the will such as, "I give up my desire for (security, esteem, control)!"[2] The effort to dis-

---

1. Cf. Appendix A: The Active Prayer.
2. Cf. Keyes, *Handbook to Higher Consciousness*, Chapters 14 and 15.

mantle the false self and the daily practice of contemplative prayer are the two engines of your spiritual jet that give you the thrust to get off the ground. The reason that centering prayer is not as effective as it could be is that when you emerge from it into the ordinary routines of daily life, your emotional programs start going off again. Upsetting emotions immediately start to drain the reservoir of interior silence, that you had established during prayer. On the other hand, if you work at dismantling the energy centers that cause the upsetting emotions, your efforts will extend the good effects of centering into every aspect of daily life.

6. *Practice guard of the heart.* This is the practice of releasing upsetting emotions into the present moment. This can be done in one of three ways: doing what you are actually doing, turning your attention to some other occupation, or giving the feeling to Christ. The guard of the heart requires the prompt letting go of personal likes or dislikes. When something arises independently of our plans, we spontaneously try to modify it. Our first reaction, however, should be openness to what is actually happening so that if our plans are upset, we are not upset. The fruit of guard of the heart is the habitual willingness to change our plans at a moment's notice. It disposes us to accept painful situations as they arise. Then we can decide what to do with them, modifying, correcting or improving them. In other words, the ordinary events of daily life become our practice. I can't emphasize that too much. A monastic structure is not the path to holiness for lay folks. The routine of daily life is. Contemplative prayer is aimed at transforming daily life with its never-ending round of ordinary activities.

7. *Practice unconditional acceptance of others.* This practice is especially powerful in quieting the emotions of the utility appetite: fear, anger, courage, hope, and despair. By accepting other people unconditionally, you discipline the emotions that want to get even with others or to get away from them. You allow people to be who they are with all their idiosyncracies and with the particular behavior that is disturbing you. The situation gets more complicated when you feel an obligation to correct someone. If you correct someone when you are upset, you are certain to get nowhere. This arouses the defenses of others and gives them a handle for blaming the situation on you. Wait till you have calmed down and then offer correction out of genuine concern for them.

8. *Deliberately dismantle excessive group identification.* This is the practice of letting go of our cultural conditioning, preconceived ideas, and over-identification with the values of our particular group. It also means openness to change in ourselves, openness to spiritual development beyond group loyalties, openness to whatever the future holds.

9. *Celebrate the Eucharist regularly.* Participate regularly in the mystery of Christ's passion, death, and resurrection, the source of Christian transformation.

10. *Join a contemplative prayer group.* Set up or join a support group that meets weekly to do centering prayer and *lectio divina* together and to encourage one another in the commitment to the contemplative dimensions of the Gospel.[3]

BASIC TOOLS FOR TIMES OF TEMPTATION

1. Determination to persevere in the spiritual journey.

2. Trust in the infinite mercy of God.

3. Continuous practice of the presence of God through prayer and openness to His inspirations.

3. Cf. Appendix B: The Weekly Support Group.

CHAPTER THIRTEEN

Guidelines for Christian Life, Growth and Transformation

The following principles represent a tentative effort to restate the Christian spiritual journey in contemporary terms. They are designed to provide a conceptual background for the practice of centering prayer. They should be read according to the method of *lectio divina*.

1. The fundamental goodness of human nature, like the mystery of the Trinity, Grace, and the Incarnation, is an essential element of Christian faith. This basic core of goodness is capable of unlimited development; indeed, of becoming transformed into Christ and deified.

2. Our basic core of goodness is our true Self. Its center of gravity is God. The acceptance of our basic goodness is a quantum leap in the spiritual journey.

3. God and our true Self are not separate. Though we are not God, God and our true Self are the same thing.

4. The term *original sin* is a way of describing the human condition, which is the universal experience of coming to full reflective self-consciousness without the certitude of personal union with God. This gives rise to our intimate sense of incompletion, dividedness, isolation, and guilt.

5. Original sin is not the result of personal wrongdoing on our part.

Still, it causes a pervasive feeling of alienation from God, from other people and from the true Self. The cultural consequences of these alienations are instilled in us from earliest childhood and passed on from one generation to the next. The urgent need to escape from the profound insecurity of this situation gives rise, when unchecked, to insatiable desires for pleasure, possession, and power. On the social level, it gives rise to violence, war, and institutional injustice.

6.   The particular consequences of original sin include all the self-serving habits that have been woven into our personality from the time we were conceived; all the emotional damage that has come from our early environment and upbringing; all the harm that other people have done to us knowingly or unknowingly at an age when we could not defend ourselves; and the methods we acquired—many of them now unconscious—to ward off the pain of unbearable situations.

7.   This constellation of prerational reactions is the foundation of the false self. The false self develops in opposition to the true Self. Its center of gravity is itself.

8.   Grace is the presence and action of Christ at every moment of our lives. The sacraments are ritual actions in which Christ is present in a special manner, confirming and sustaining the major commitments of our Christian life.

9.   In Baptism, the false self is ritually put to death, the new self is born, and the victory over sin won by Jesus through his death and resurrection is placed at our disposal. Not our uniqueness as persons, but our sense of separation from God and from others is destroyed in the death-dealing and life-giving waters of Baptism.

10.   The Eucharist is the celebration of life: the coming together of all the material elements of the cosmos, their emergence to consciousness in human persons and the transformation of human consciousness into Divine consciousness. It is the manifestation of the Divine in and through the Christian community. We receive the Eucharist in order to become the Eucharist.

11.   In addition to being present in the sacraments, Christ is present in a special manner in every crisis and important event of our lives.

12. Personal sin is the refusal to respond to Christ's self-communication (grace). It is the deliberate neglect of our own genuine needs and those of others. It reinforces the false self.

13. Our basic core of goodness is dynamic and tends to grow of itself. This growth is hindered by the illusions and emotional hang-ups of the false self, by the negative influences coming from our cultural condition-ing, and by personal sin.

14. Listening to God's word in scripture and the liturgy, waiting upon God in prayer, and responsiveness to his inspirations help to distinguish how the two selves are operating in particular circumstances.

15. God is not some remote, inaccessible, and implacable Being who demands instant perfection from His creatures and of whose love we must make ourselves worthy. He is not a tyrant to be obeyed out of terror, nor a policeman who is ever on the watch, nor a harsh judge ever ready to apply the verdict of guilty. We should relate to Him less and less in terms of reward and punishment and more and more on the basis of the gratuity—or the *play* of divine love.

16. Divine love is compassionate, tender, luminous, totally self-giving, seeking no reward, unifying everything.

17. The experience of being loved by God enables us to accept our false self as it is, and then to let go of it and journey to our true Self. The inward journey to our true Self is the way to divine love.

18. The growing awareness of our true Self, along with the deep sense of spiritual peace and joy which flow from this experience, balances the psychic pain of the disintegrating and dying of the false self. As the moti-vating power of the false self diminishes, our true Self builds the *new self* with the motivating force of divine love.

19. The building of our *new self* is bound to be marked by innumerable mistakes and sometimes by sin. Such failures, however serious, are insignifi-cant compared to the inviolable goodness of our true Self. We should ask God's pardon, seek forgiveness from those we may have offended, and then act with renewed confidence and energy as if nothing had happened.

20. Prolonged, pervasive, or paralyzing guilt feelings come from the false self. True guilt in response to personal sin or social injustice does not

lead to discouragement but to amendment of life. It is a call to conversion.

21.   Progress in the spiritual journey is manifested by the uncondi-tional acceptance of other people, beginning with those with whom we live.

22.   A community of faith offers the support of example, correction, and mutual concern in the spiritual journey. Above all, participating in the mystery of Christ through the celebration of the liturgy, Eucharist, and silent prayer binds the community in a common search for transformation and union with God. The presence of Christ is ministered to each other and becomes tangible in the community, especially when it is gathered for worship or engaged in some work of service to those in need.

23.   The moderation of the instinctual drives of the developing human organism for survival and security, affection and esteem, control and power allows true human needs to come into proper focus. Primary among these needs is intimacy with another or several human persons. By intimacy is meant the mutual sharing of thoughts, feelings, problems, and spiritual aspirations which gradually develops into spiritual friendship.

24.   Spiritual friendship involving genuine self-disclosure is an essential ingredient for happiness both in marriage and in the celibate lifestyle. The experience of intimacy with another or several persons expands and deepens our capacity to relate to God and to everyone else. Under the influence of Divine Love the sexual energy is gradually transformed into universal compassion.

25.   The spiritual radiation of a community depends on the commit-ment of its members to the inward journey and to each other. To offer one another space in which to grow as persons is an integral part of this commitment.

26.   Contemplative prayer, in the traditional sense of the term, is the dynamic that initiates, accompanies and brings the process of transforma-tion to completion.

27.   Reflection on the Word of God in scripture and in our personal history is the foundation of contemplative prayer. The spontaneous let-ting go of particular thoughts and feelings in prayer is a sign of progress in contemplation. Contemplative prayer is characterized not so much by the absence of thoughts and feelings as by detachment from them.

28.   The goal of genuine spiritual practice is not the rejection of the good things of the body, mind, or spirit, but the right use of them. No aspect of human nature or period of human life is to be rejected but integrated into each successive level of unfolding self-consciousness. In this way, the partial goodness proper to each stage of human development is preserved and only its limitations are left behind. The way to become divine is thus to become fully human.

29.   The practice of a spiritual discipline is essential at the beginning of the spiritual journey as a means of developing the foundations of the contemplative dimension of life: dedication and devotion to God and service to others. Our daily practice should include a time for contemplative prayer and a program for letting go of the false self.

30.   Regular periods of silence and solitude quiet the psyche, foster interior silence, and initiate the dynamic of self-knowledge.

31.   Solitude is not primarily a place but an attitude of total commitment to God. When one belongs completely to God, the sharing of one's life and gifts continually increases.

32.   The Beatitude of poverty of spirit springs from the increasing awareness of our true Self. It is a nonpossessive attitude toward everything and a sense of unity with everything at the same time. The interior freedom to have much or to have little, and the simplifying of one's life-style are signs of the presence of poverty of spirit.

33.   Chastity is distinct from celibacy, which is the commitment to abstain from the genital expression of our sexuality. Chastity is the acceptance of our sexual energy, together with the masculine and feminine qualities that accompany it and the integration of this energy into our spirituality. It is the practice of moderation and self-control in the use of our sexual energy.

34.   Chastity enhances and expands the power to love. It perceives the sacredness of everything that is. As a consequence, one respects the dignity of other persons and cannot use them merely for one's own fulfillment.

35.   Obedience is the unconditional acceptance of God as He is and as He manifests Himself in our lives. God's will is not immediately evident. Docility inclines us to attend to all the indications of His will. Dis-

cernment sifts the evidence and then decides, in the light of the inward attraction of grace, what God seems to be asking here and now.

36.   Humility is an attitude of honesty with God, oneself, and all reality. It enables us to be at peace in the presence of our powerlessness and to rest in the forgetfulness of self.

37.   Hope springs from the continuing experience of God's compassion and help. Patience is hope in action. It waits for the saving help of God without giving up, giving in, or going away, and for any length of time.

38.   The disintegrating and dying of our false self is our participation in the passion and death of Jesus. The building of our *new self*, based on the transforming power of divine love, is our participation in his risen life.

39.   In the beginning, emotional hang-ups are the chief obstacle to the growth of our *new self* because they put our freedom into a straight jacket. Later, because of the subtle satisfaction that springs from self-control, spiritual pride becomes the chief obstacle. And finally, reflection of self becomes the chief obstacle because this hinders the innocence of divine union.

40.   Human effort depends on grace even as it invites it. Whatever degree of divine union we may reach bears no proportion to our effort. It is the sheer gift of divine love.

41.   Jesus did not teach a specific method of meditation or bodily discipline for quieting the imagination, memory, and emotions. We should choose a spiritual practice adapted to our particular temperament and natural disposition. We must also be willing to dispense with it when called by the Spirit to surrender to his direct guidance. The Spirit is above every method or practice. To follow his inspiration is the sure path to perfect freedom.

42.   What Jesus proposed to his disciples as the Way is his own example: the forgiveness of everything and everyone and the service of others in their needs. "Love one another as I have loved you."

APPENDICES

THE ACTIVE PRAYER

The sacred word is designed to lead into silence. Hence, it should be short—one or two syllables. The active prayer—an aspiration drawn from scripture for use in daily life—should be longer—five to nine syllables. The saying of the syllables is synchronized with one's heartbeat. While some people like to use a variety of aspirations for this purpose, it is easier to work a single aspiration into the subconscious. The great advantage of this practice is that it eventually becomes a "tape" similar to the "tapes" that accompany one's upsetting emotions. When this occurs, the aspiration has the remarkable effect of erasing the old tapes, thus providing a neutral zone in which common sense or the Spirit of God can suggest what should be done.

The active prayer has to be repeated again and again at free moments in order to work it into the subconscious. The old tapes were built up through repeated acts. A new tape can be established in the same way. It may take a year to establish one's active prayer in the subconscious. It will then arise spontaneously. One may wake up saying it or it may accompany one's dreams.

Go about this practice without anxiety, haste, or excessive effort. Do not blame yourself for forgetting to say it on some days; just start up again.

It should not be repeated when your mind is occupied with other things such as conversation, study, or work requiring concentration.

Following are examples of active prayer.

O Lord, come to my assistance.

O God, make haste to help me.

Holy Mary, Mother of God.

Abide in my love.

My God and My All.

My Jesus, mercy.

Kyrie Eleison.

Veni Sancti Spiritus.

Gloria in excelsis Deo.

Agnus Dei, dona nobis pacem.

I belong to you, O Lord.

Soul of Christ, sanctify me.

Take, Lord, and receive all I have.

Bless the Lord, my soul.

Open my heart to your love.

Lord, I give myself to you.

My Lord and my God.

Body of Christ, save me.

Lord increase my faith.

Not my will but thine be done.

Thy kingdom come, Thy will be done.

Open my heart to your love.

Jesus, my light and my love.

May my being praise you, Lord.

Through Him, with Him, in Him.

Jesus, my light and my love.

Our help is in the name of the Lord.

Holy Spirit, pray in me.

Lord, do with me what You will.

Speak Lord, Your servant is listening.

THE WEEKLY SUPPORT GROUP

While centering prayer is done privately most of the time, a weekly sharing of the experience in a small group (up to fifteen) has proven to be very supportive, as well as a means of continuing education. The weekly meeting also serves as a means of accountability. Just knowing that one's support group is meeting together each week is an enormous encouragement to keep going, or an invitation to return to the practice of centering prayer if circumstances such as illness, business, family problems, or urgent duties have prevented one from carrying out one's commitment to daily practice for a time.

By sharing the experience of centering prayer with others, one's own discernment of the ups and downs of the practice is sharpened. The group serves as a source of encouragement and can normally solve problems that might arise regarding the method. The collective discernment of the group tends to be well balanced.

Following is the format suggested for the weekly meeting.

Setting: Chairs placed in a circle.

Format:

1. A slow, meditative walk in silence, moving in single file in a circle around the room. Each one joins the circle as he or she arrives. Walk for about ten minutes.

2. A brief office, or chanting (four or five minutes).

3. Centering prayer period. Choose one of the following:
   a. Twenty-minute sit.
   b. Two twenty-minute sits with contemplative walk in between. In both cases end with a slow recitation of "Our Father" by the leader or two minutes of silence to return to ordinary thinking.

4. *Lectio divina*: In the beginning, the "Guidelines for Christian Life, Growth, and Transformation" (Chapter Thirteen) may be used as a means of developing a conceptual background for the practice of centering prayer. Discuss in the group how each guideline may relate to each one's own life experience. Or use scriptural texts or readings from books on contemplative prayer. Allow half an hour or forty-five minutes for this period of sharing. Avoid theological, philosophical, or scriptural debates.

The purpose of the meeting is spiritual refreshment and mutual encouragement in the practice.

A MEDITATION

We begin our prayer by disposing our body. Let it be relaxed and calm, but inwardly alert.

The root of prayer is interior silence. We may think of prayer as thoughts or feelings expressed in words. But this is only one expression. Deep prayer is the laying aside of thoughts. It is the opening of mind and heart, body and feelings—our whole being—to God, the Ultimate Mystery, beyond words, thoughts, and emotions. We do not resist them or suppress them. We accept them as they are and go beyond them, not by effort, but by letting them all go by. We open our awareness to the Ultimate Mystery whom we know by faith is within us, closer than breathing, closer than thinking, closer than choosing—closer than consciousness itself. The Ultimate Mystery is the ground in which our being is rooted, the Source from whom our life emerges at every moment.

We are totally present now, with the whole of our being, in complete openness, in deep prayer. The past and future—time itself—are forgotten. We are here in the presence of the Ultimate Mystery. Like the air we breathe, this divine Presence is all around us and within us, distinct from us, but never separate from us. We may sense this Presence drawing us from within, as if touching our spirit and embracing it, or carrying us beyond ourselves into pure awareness.

We surrender to the attraction of interior silence, tranquility, and peace. We do not try to feel anything, reflect about anything. Without effort, without trying, we sink into this Presence, letting everything else go. Let love alone speak: the simple desire to be one with the Presence, to forget self, and to rest in the Ultimate Mystery.

This Presence is immense, yet so humble; awe-inspiring, yet so gentle; limitless, yet so intimate, tender and personal. I *know* that I am *known*. Everything in my life is transparent in this Presence. It knows everything about me—all my weaknesses, brokenness, sinfulness—and still loves me infinitely. This Presence is healing, strengthening, refreshing—just by its Presence. It is nonjudgmental, self-giving, seeking no reward, boundless in compassion. It is like coming home to a place I should never have left, to an awareness that was somehow always there, but which I did not recognize. I cannot force this awareness, or bring it about. A door opens within me, but from the other side. I seem to have tasted before the mysterious sweetness of this enveloping, permeating Presence. It is both emptiness and fullness at once.

We wait patiently; in silence, openness, and quiet attentiveness; motionless within and without. We surrender to the attraction to be still, to be loved, just to *be*.

How shallow are all the things that upset and discourage me! I resolve to give up the desires that trigger my tormenting emotions. Having tasted true peace, I can let them all go by. Of course, I shall stumble and fall, for I know my weakness. But I will rise at once, for I know my goal. I know where my home *is*.

THE ESSENTIALS OF THE CENTERING PRAYER METHOD

Theological Background

The grace of Pentecost affirms that the risen Jesus is among us as the glorified Christ. Christ lives in each of us as the Enlightened One, present everywhere and at all times. He is the living Master who continuously sends the Holy Spirit to dwell within us and to bear witness to his resurrection by empowering us to experience and manifest the fruits of the Spirit and the Beatitudes both in prayer and action.

Lectio Divina

Lectio divina is the most traditional way of cultivating friendship with Christ. It is a way of listening to the texts of scripture as if we were in conversation with Christ and he were suggesting the topics of conversation. The daily encounter with Christ and reflection on his word leads beyond mere acquaintanceship to an attitude of friendship, trust, and love. Conversation simplifies and gives way to communing, or as Gregory the Great (sixth century), summarizing the Christian contemplative tradition, put it, "resting in God." This was the classical meaning of contemplative prayer for the first sixteen centuries.

Contemplative Prayer

Contemplative prayer is the normal development of the grace of baptism and the regular practice of *lectio divina*. We may think of prayer as thoughts or feelings expressed in words. But this is only one expression. Contemplative prayer is the opening of mind and heart—our whole being—to God, the Ultimate Mystery, beyond thoughts, words, and emotions. We open our awareness to God whom we know by faith is within us, closer than breathing, closer than thinking, closer than choosing—closer than consciousness itself. Contemplative prayer is a process of interior purification leading, if we consent, to divine union.

The Method of Centering Prayer

Centering prayer is a method designed to deepen the relationship with Christ begun in *lectio divina* and to facilitate the development of contemplative prayer by preparing our faculties to cooperate with this gift. It is an attempt to present the teaching of earlier times (e.g., *The Cloud of Unknowing*) in an updated form and to put a certain order and regularity into it. It is not meant to replace other kinds of prayer; it simply puts other kinds of prayer into a new and fuller perspective. During the time of prayer, we consent to God's presence and action within. At other times our attention moves outward to discover God's presence everywhere else.

The Guidelines

1. Choose a sacred word as the symbol of your intention to consent to God's presence and action within.

2. Sitting comfortably and with eyes closed, settle briefly, and silently introduce the sacred word as the symbol of your consent to God's presence and action within.

3. When you become aware of thoughts, return ever-so-gently to the sacred word.

4. At the end of the prayer period, remain in silence with eyes closed for a couple of minutes.

Explanation of the Guidelines

1. "Choose a sacred word as the symbol of your intention to consent to God's presence and action within" (see Chapter Five).
      a. The sacred word expresses our intention to be in God's presence and to yield to the divine action.
      b. The sacred word should be chosen during a brief period of prayer asking the Holy Spirit to inspire us with one that is especially suitable for us.
          1. Examples: Lord, Jesus, Abba, Father, Mother.
          2. Other possibilities: Love, Peace, Shalom, Silence.

    c. Having chosen a sacred word, we do not change it during the prayer period, for that would be to start thinking again.

    d. A simple inward gaze upon God may be more suitable for some persons than the sacred word. In this case, one consents to God's presence and action by turning inwardly toward God as if gazing upon him. The same guidelines apply to the sacred gaze as to the sacred word.

2. "Sitting comfortably and with eyes closed, settle briefly, and silently introduce the sacred word as the symbol of your consent to God's presence and action within."

    a. By "sitting comfortably" is meant relatively comfortably; not so comfortably that we encourage sleep, but sitting comfortably enough to avoid thinking about the discomfort of our bodies during this time of prayer.

    b. Whatever sitting position we choose, we keep the back straight.

    c. If we fall asleep, we continue the prayer for a few minutes upon awakening if we can spare the time.

    d. Praying in this way after a main meal encourages drowsiness. Better to wait an hour at least before centering prayer. Praying in this way just before retiring may disturb one's sleep pattern.

    e. We close our eyes to let go of what is going on around and within us.

    f. We introduce the sacred word inwardly and as gently as laying a feather on a piece of absorbent cotton.

3. "When you become aware of thoughts, return ever-so-gently to the sacred word."

    a. "Thoughts" is an umbrella term for every perception including sense perceptions, feelings, images, memories, reflections, and commentaries.

    b. Thoughts are a normal part of centering prayer.

    c. By "returning ever-so-gently to the sacred word," a minimum of effort is indicated. This is the only activity we initiate during the time of centering prayer.

    d. During the course of our prayer, the sacred word may become vague or even disappear.

4. "At the end of the prayer period, remain in silence with eyes closed for two or three minutes."

    a. If this prayer is done in a group, the leader may slowly recite the Our Father during the additional two or three minutes while the others listen.

    b. The additional two or three minutes give the psyche time to readjust to the external senses and enable us to bring the atmosphere of silence into daily life.

Some Practical Points

1. The minimum time for this prayer is twenty minutes. Two periods are recommended each day, one first thing in the morning, and one in the afternoon or early evening.

2. The end of the prayer period can be indicated by a timer, provided it does not have an audible tick or loud sound when it goes off.

3. The principal effects of centering prayer are experienced in daily life, not in the period of centering prayer itself.

4. Physical symptoms:

    a. We may notice slight pains, itches, or twitches in various parts of the body, or a generalized restlessness. These are usually due to the untying of emotional knots in the body.

    b. We may also notice heaviness or lightness in the extremities. This is usually due to a deep level of spiritual attentiveness.

    c. In either case, we pay no attention, or we allow the mind to rest briefly in the sensation and then return to the sacred word.

5. *Lectio divina* provides the conceptual background for the development of centering prayer.

6. A support group praying and sharing together once a week helps maintain one's commitment to the prayer.

Extending the Effects of Centering Prayer into Daily Life

1. Practice two periods of centering prayer daily.

2. Read scriptures regularly and study the parts of this book that deal with the method.

3. Practice one or two of the specific practices for everyday life suggested in Chapter Twelve.

4. Join a Centering Prayer Support Group or Follow-up Program (if available in your area).
    a. The group meeting encourages the members of the group to persevere in private.
    b. It also provides an opportunity for further input on a regular basis through tapes, readings, and discussion.

Points for Further Development

1. During the prayer period, various kinds of thoughts may be distinguished (see Chapters Six through Ten):
    a. Ordinary wanderings of the imagination or memory.
    b. Thoughts that give rise to attractions or aversions.
    c. Insights and psychological breakthroughs.
    d. Self-reflections such as, "How am I doing?" or "This peace is just great!"
    e. Thoughts that arise from the unloading of the unconscious.

2. During this prayer, we avoid analyzing our experience, harboring expectations, or aiming at some specific goal such as the following:
    a. Repeating the sacred word continuously.
    b. Having no thoughts.
    c. Making the mind a blank.
    d. Feeling peaceful or consoled.
    e. Achieving a spiritual experience.

3. What centering prayer is not:
    a. It is not a technique.
    b. It is not a relaxation exercise.
    c. It is not a form of self-hypnosis.

    d. It is not a charismatic gift.

    e. It is not a parapsychological phenomenon.

    f. It is not limited to the "felt" presence of God.

    g. It is not discursive meditation or affective prayer.

4. What centering prayer is:

    a. It is at the same time a relationship with God and a discipline to foster that relationship.

    b. It is an exercise of faith, hope, and love.

    c. It is a movement beyond conversation with Christ to communion.

    d. It habituates us to the language of God which is silence.

A BRIEF HISTORY OF CONTEMPLATIVE OUTREACH

Centering Prayer

During the first sixteen centuries of Church history, contemplative prayer was the acknowledged goal of Christian spirituality for clergy and laity alike. After the Reformation, this heritage, at least as a living tradition, was virtually lost. Now in the twentieth century with the advent of cross-cultural dialogue and historical research, the recovery of the Christian contemplative tradition has begun. The method of centering prayer, in the context of the tradition of *lectio divina*, is contributing to this renewal.

Throughout the 1970s, a group of Trappist monks continued this search at St. Joseph's Abbey in Spencer, Massachusetts. In 1975 the contemplative practice called centering prayer, based on the fourteenth century classic *The Cloud of Unknowing*, was developed by Frs. William Menninger and Basil Pennington. This method of prayer was offered at the guest house in Spencer first to priests and later to lay people. The response was so positive that an increasing number of workshops was offered and an advanced workshop was developed by Fr. Thomas Keating to train teachers of the method.

Contemplative Outreach

In 1981, Fr. Keating resigned as abbot of St. Joseph's and moved to St. Benedict's Monastery in Snowmass, Colorado. Requests to share centering prayer in various parts of the country as well as requests for a more intensive centering prayer experience began to surface. In 1983 the first Intensive Centering Prayer Retreat was held at the Lama Foundation in San Cristobal, New Mexico. Since then, Intensives have been given at St. Benedict's Monastery in Snowmass and in several other locations. Two Post-Intensive Retreats are held each year and Formation Weeks are given.

Organization

Because of the growing interest in centering prayer in certain areas of the country, a number of local centering prayer support groups grew up and soon the need to organize became evident.

In 1984, Contemplative Outreach, Ltd. was established to coordinate efforts to introduce the centering prayer method to persons seeking a deeper life of prayer and to provide a support system capable of sustaining their commitment. In 1986, a national office of Contemplative Outreach was established.

Communities

Presently there are thirty-seven active regions including international areas. Chrysalis House, a live-in community in Warwick, New York, established in 1985, offers formation in centering prayer and contemplative living.

For information and resources, contact the national office:
Contemplative Outreach, Ltd., 9 William Street, P.O. Box 737, Butler, NJ 07405   Tel.: (201) 838-3384

GLOSSARY OF TERMS

Apophatic/Kataphatic contemplation—a misleading distinction suggesting opposition between the two; in fact, a proper preparation of the faculties (kataphatic practice) leads to apophatic contemplation, which in turn is sustained through appropriate kataphatic practices.

    a) Apophatic (darksome)—the exercise of pure faith; resting in God beyond concepts and particular acts, except to maintain a general loving attention to the divine presence.

    b) Kataphatic (lightsome)—the exercise of the rational faculties enlightened by faith: the affective response to symbols, reflection, and the use of reason, imagination, and memory in order to assimilate the truths of faith.

Attention—the focusing on a particular object such as God's word in scripture, the breath, an image, or a concept.

Awareness—the act of being aware of a particular or general perception; another term for consciousness.

Beatitudes (Matt. 5:1–10)—a further development of the fruits of the Spirit.

Centering prayer—a contemporary form of prayer of the heart, prayer of simplicity, prayer of faith, prayer of simple regard; a method of reducing the obstacles to the gift of contemplative prayer and of facilitating the development of habits conducive to responding to the inspirations of the Spirit.

Consent—an act of the will expressing acceptance of someone, some thing, or some course of action; the manifestation of one's intention.

Contemplation—a synonym for contemplative prayer.

Contemplative living—activity in daily life prompted by the Gifts of the Spirit; the fruit of a contemplative attitude.

Contemplative prayer—the development of one's relationship with Christ to the point of communing beyond words, thoughts, feelings, and the multiplication of particular acts; a process moving from the simplified activity of waiting upon God to the ever-increasing predominance of the Gifts of the Spirit as the source of one's prayer.

Contemplative walk—a slow meditative walk of five to seven minutes recommended when two or more periods of centering prayer are held back-to-back. Its purpose is to dissipate the restlessness that may build up as a result of remaining in one position for a longer time than one is used to, and to provide an opportunity to bring the interior peace of contemplative prayer into a simple form of activity.

Divine union—a term describing a single experience of the union of all the faculties in God or the permanent state of union called transforming union.

Ecstacy—the temporary suspension by the divine action of the thinking and feeling faculties, including at times the external senses, which facilitates the experience of divine union.

Fruits of the Spirit (Gal. 4:22–24)—nine aspects of "the mind of Christ" manifesting the growth of the divine life in us.

False self—the self developed in our own likeness rather than in the likeness of God; the self-image developed to cope with the emotional trauma of early childhood, which seeks happiness in satisfying the instinctual needs of survival/security, affection/esteem, and power/control, and which bases its self-worth on cultural or group identification.

Gifts of the Spirit—

a. Charismatic gifts of the Spirit (1 Cor. 12:1–13)—given primarily to encourage the Christian community.

b. Seven Gifts of the Spirit (Is. 11:2)—habitual dispositions empowering us to perceive and follow the promptings of the Holy Spirit both in prayer and action.

Intention—the choice of the will in regard to some goal or purpose.

Interior silence—the quieting of the imagination, feelings, and rational faculties in the process of recollection; the general, loving attentiveness to God in pure faith.

Lectio divina—reading or more exactly, listening to the book we believe to be divinely inspired; the most ancient method of developing the friendship of Christ by using scripture texts as topics of conversation with Christ.

Method of contemplative prayer—any prayer practice that spontaneously evolves or is deliberately designed to free the mind of excessive dependence on thinking to go to God.

a. Practices spontaneously evolving toward contemplation—*lectio divina*, the Jesus Prayer, Veneration of Icons, the Rosary, and most other traditional devotions of the Church rightly used.

b. Practices deliberately designed to facilitate contemplation—

1. Concentrative—the Jesus Prayer, mantric practice (constant repetition of a word or phrase), Dom John Main's method of contemplative prayer.

2. Receptive—centering prayer, prayer of faith, prayer of the heart, prayer of simplicity, prayer of silence, prayer of simple regard, active recollection, acquired contemplation.

c. On a scale of 1 to 10, some practices are more concentrative, others more receptive.

Mystical prayer—a synonym for contemplative prayer.

Mysticism—a synonym for contemplation.

Purification—an essential part of the process of contemplation through which the dark side of one's personality, mixed motivation, and the emotional pain of a lifetime stored in the unconscious are gradually evacuated; the necessary preparation for transforming union.

Spiritual attentiveness—the general loving attention to the presence of God in pure faith, whether an undifferentiated sense of unity or a more personal attention to one or other of the Divine Persons.

Thoughts—in the context of the specific method of centering prayer, an umbrella term for any perception at all, including sense perceptions, feelings, images, memories, reflections, commentaries, and particular spiritual perceptions.

Transformation (transforming union)—the stable conviction of the abiding presence of God rather than a particular experience or set of experiences; a restructuring of consciousness in which the divine reality is perceived to be present in oneself and in all that is.

True Self—the image of God in which every human being is created; our participation in the divine life manifested in our uniqueness.

Ultimate Mystery/Ultimate Reality—the ground of infinite potentiality and actualization; a term emphasizing the divine transcendence.

Unloading the unconscious—the coming to awareness of previously unconscious emotional material from early childhood in the form of primitive feelings or a barrage of images, especially during the time of prayer.